THE
7
QUESTIONS

THE
7
QUESTIONS

*The Ultimate Toolkit to Boost
Self-Esteem, Unlock Your Potential
and Transform Your Life*

NICK HATTER

PIATKUS

PIATKUS

First published in Great Britain in 2022 by Piatkus

1 3 5 7 9 10 8 6 4 2

A CIP catalogue record for this book
is available from the British Library.

ISBN: 978-0-349-42881-9

Typeset in Caslon by M Rules
Printed and bound in Great Britain by
Clays Ltd, Elcograf S.p.A.

Papers used by Piatkus are from well-managed forests
and other responsible sources.

Piatkus
An imprint of
Little, Brown Book Group
Carmelite House
50 Victoria Embankment
London EC4Y 0DZ

An Hachette UK Company
www.hachette.co.uk

www.littlebrown.co.uk

Dedicated to my fellows in recovery,
my mother, my best friend, Steve,
and the FDBK team.

Contents

Introduction

'What is necessary to change a person is to change his awareness of himself.'

—ABRAHAM MASLOW

Caution: This book isn't like other self-help titles. Read the introduction

Usually, when I pick up a self-help book, I immediately skip to Chapter 1, because who has time for reading or listening to introductions nowadays? There are things to do, demands to meet, goals to achieve, and places to get to. Of course, *being busy and being productive are not the same thing.* I often treat self-help books the same way I treat new appliances; I just want them to work, and I don't have time to read the instructions. Inevitably, I later regret not reading them when they would have saved me hours of figuring out why the appliance doesn't work. So as tempting as it is to skip ahead, I invite you to *slow down* first and take the time to learn more about the journey you are about to embark on with this book. Stop the busyness and rushing. This time is for *you*, and you alone. Turn off the phone, get off social media, pour yourself a chamomile tea, take a deep breath, and mindfully read this introduction – because you need to understand what this book is about, why I wrote it and how it's going to help you change your life. *You are worth investing time in.*

Self-awareness is the key to personal transformation

What if I told you that there were 7 simple questions that could transform your life? Well, the good news is that there are – and they're called *The 7 Questions*, which have been expertly distilled from over thirteen years of experience in personal development. This includes numerous forms of mentoring, coaching, psychotherapy and addiction recovery programmes I have undergone myself, as well as years of training in various styles of coaching and solution-focused psychotherapy. This is in addition to several years of coaching and supporting others and helping them change their lives. Throughout my journey, I discovered the vital component behind personal growth: *self-awareness.* And one of the best ways to get more of this is by asking yourself questions.

From 2018, I collected data from over 350 client consultations where I would have prospective coachees complete a form to indicate what they were struggling with, and I discovered the most common reasons why people were seeking out a life coach like me. From least to most common, these were:

10. Not enough money
9. Difficult emotions (anger, fear, sadness, etc.)
8. Relationship issues
7. Unable to reach the next level in their career
6. Boredom and unfulfilment
5. Low motivation
4. Procrastination
3. Low confidence or low self-esteem
2. Unsure of career direction and purpose
1. Not living the life they wanted

Time and again in my coaching practice, I found myself asking a similar set of deep questions to help clients address these particular issues. As a result of asking some of these questions, I have seen my clients transform their thinking and their lives. Even today, I ask myself these questions again and again in my head – and every time I do, I often get new insights and more growth, which has empowered me to become a better version of myself. If you are open, honest and willing, then these questions will also have a profound effect on your life.

While advice can be useful or even necessary in some contexts, by itself, it makes it hard to access self-awareness, as it's generally take it or leave it. Questions, however, force you to look within and help you to gain self-awareness. Typically, self-help books offer lots of advice and make you feel better or more motivated – temporarily. They generally offer *rules* or *habits*. There is certainly no shortage of such books in the self-help world. In fact, I would go as far to say it's become saturated with such books; *do this, do that, don't do this, don't do that*, and so forth. Unfortunately, often such guidance goes in one ear, and out the other. This is not the case with *The 7 Questions*. Instead, this book will ask you a series of questions to help you discover and understand yourself like never before. In my experience, it can be much more powerful when a client reflects on a question and has an 'aha' moment rather than me providing them with the answer. Of course, some questions are hard to answer – especially if they are very deep ones. So to help you along the way, I will provide plenty of support by sharing some of the most helpful and insightful answers to these questions as well as further prompts and other points to consider to help you discover your own unique answers.

Suppose you're drunk and throwing up at 3 a.m. on a Saturday. One of the fundamental questions in life at that moment might be, 'What on *earth* was in that kebab?' Of course, it had absolutely *nothing* to do with the six pints or cocktails you had beforehand – it was *definitely* the kebab! At other times, there are powerful and deep questions you need to ask yourself (while stone-cold sober) if you want to transform your life and be your best self. There are questions which, if you ask them with an open mind, will be especially helpful if you are experiencing a dilemma or crisis, such as losing a job or financial hardship, are going through a break-up, or are going through a mid- (or quarter-) life crisis, and so forth – or if you simply want to grow as a person and achieve your full potential.

Why should you listen to me?

I am one of the highest-rated life coaches in the UK, and I have been consulted as an expert by leading magazines and news-papers, as well as appearing on national radio and TV numerous times. In addition, I am one of the few life coaches in the UK who is trusted by psychology and medical professionals, includ-ing doctors, neuroscientists, psychiatrists, therapists and clinical psychologists.

I have coached and helped a wide range of clients, from celebrities, TV presenters, actors, CEOs, lawyers, accountants, to ex-military, stay-at-home mums and even homeless people. Oxford psychiatrist and neuroscience champion Dr Shah Tarfarosh is a fan of 'preventative psychiatry' (helping people *before* they have severe mental health issues) who recognises that life coaches like me are doing 'vital work' in helping those who may not necessarily be clinically depressed, but suffer from 'miserable life syndrome'. I concur; I have helped people who suffered from myriad problems such as low self-confidence, feel-ing stuck in their life or in their career, and had I not intervened when I did, they may have ended up needing more serious psychiatric support such as antidepressants.

Aside from my professional training, I also have vast personal first-hand experience; I'm not an 'armchair psychologist'. I struggled with low self-esteem throughout much of my life and have battled trauma and multiple addictions. I grew up in a very chaotic and dysfunctional home where I faced much emotional (and sometimes physical) abuse and shame. I went to one of the roughest schools in Bristol where I was severely bullied and was very unpopular. I was also bullied and isolated at college and even at university. I previously had hardly any boundaries and self-respect.

People have talked down to me a lot in life, and I was very much a 'yes man' and a people pleaser. I never considered myself much of a ladies' man either; I faced much rejection and unrequited love. In fact, the first girl I ever fell in love with left me for my best friend! And then after that, my first long-term girlfriend of two years broke up with me and left me for another friend. Thereafter, I suffered and co-created many unhealthy and toxic relationships. I also walked away from a £1.7 million business that I had spent four years building after having a spectacular burnout and breakdown.

The gift in all of this was that these experiences led me to stay hungry for personal development and they put me on a path to improve my self-esteem. In addition to years of studying various forms of coaching and solution-focused psychotherapy, I have had several years of psychotherapy and coaching for various areas of my life for everything from entrepreneurship, marketing, sales, dating and self-defence to healthy masculinity. Psychotherapy has been amazing for my mental health and personal growth. If it wasn't for psychotherapy, I wouldn't be here today. And if it wasn't for coaching, I wouldn't be living the life I am today on a sunny beach in Gran Canaria. I am very blessed with the success of my life coaching practice, and I put a lot of this down to the life coaching I had for myself.

I also have over five years' experience in 12-Step Addiction Recovery where I have done extensive pro-bono coaching, listening and giving support to others. Note that though I may use addiction coaching as examples in this book, the principles are still widely applicable to other situations and examples.

I have learned so much about improving self-esteem – and continue to do so – all of which is valuable knowledge that I can pass on to my clients and, of course, readers like you. So, if you are suffering from low self-esteem, poor self-image, bad habits, procrastination, or are unsure of which direction to go in your life or your career, know that you are not alone and that it can and will get better. I have walked the journey of self-improvement for many years and now it's time to help you live the life you always knew you could live, and help you become the person you knew deep down you could be.

Rest assured, you are in good hands, and I thank you for your trust as we embark on this exciting journey of self-discovery together.

Why should you trust a life coach?

These days, it seems like there's no shortage of self-help gurus and life coaches. If you've ever watched the British comedy TV series *Peep Show* (starring David Mitchell and Robert Webb), then you may have realised that *anyone* can call themselves a 'life coach' and dish out questionable advice and solutions. In one *Peep Show* episode, the unscrupulous character Jez (played by Webb) becomes a life coach overnight and tells a 'client' that he fancies that they should *definitely* break up with their boyfriend. Needless to say I have strong ethical concerns about this advice, as well as the fact that Jez is coaching with his client sitting on his bed (!). That's an extreme example, of course, but it's important to get help from credible people.

I often joke that the difference between a co-dependent, a therapist and a coach is that a co-dependent tries to solve another person's problems free of charge, and that the difference between a therapist and a life coach is that the latter gets paid a lot more without having to wear tweed jackets. One of my coaching supervisors, Frances Masters, is both a therapeutic coach and accredited psychotherapist with the British Association of Counselling and Psychotherapy (BACP) with over thirty thousand professional hours experience. After having navigated the rocky road of integrating psychotherapy and coaching herself, she came to the following conclusion: *'Trying to differentiate between coaching and therapy is a bit like trying to nail jelly to a wall.'* In other words, a neat and distinct separation is difficult as there can be much overlap between the two. But in any case, I will attempt to give a broad comparison.

Life coaching, unlike therapy, is less about healing emotional trauma or treating mental health disorders and is instead about unlocking your full potential, achieving personal excellence and goals, helping you to become the very best you can be. Life coaching can be very therapeutic, but it is often more solution-focused and brief than traditional psychotherapy (which tends to be more long-term and focuses on healing trauma). Rapid personal growth while achieving personal goals, without years of crying in therapy and the unfortunate stigma that can come from people knowing you're in therapy? That's certainly a very attractive proposition to a lot of people. This may explain why, in 2020, for every four people searching for a local therapist in the UK, one person searched for a local life coach – and this number I expect will continue to grow as people don't want to keep rehashing their childhood. More therapists have certainly clocked on to this and have started training and marketing themselves as life coaches. Copycats.

What are the 7 Questions?

This book is like a Swiss Army knife; it has 7 major questions which form a self-coaching toolkit that you can apply time and again for more clarity and continuous self-awareness. The questions force you to search within yourself and address the bigger picture of your life. Each of these questions then has follow-up questions, prompts and guidance that serve as additional tools for personal growth, raising self-awareness, clarity and insight further, and also address life's challenges on a smaller and more specific 'micro' level. These tools can also be used in myriad ways which thus create *even more* tools if you're taught how. For example, a Swiss Army knife has a sharp blade which can be used for the obvious: slicing things, or perhaps maiming someone who thinks Crocs are trendy footwear.*

But it can be used for several different purposes, such as:

- Lighting a fire by striking it with a stone
- Shaving
- Cauterising and disinfecting wounds (by heating the blade)

What makes a Swiss Army knife a great toolkit is not only its versatility but also its portability and ease of use. Instead of having seven different tools jumbled haphazardly in a toolbox, a Swiss Army knife is coherently designed to make it convenient to use. As such, this book has been structured in a way that addresses your life from the inside out.

The 7 Questions are actually more like 42+ questions. But carrying 42 tools around would be exhausting, awkward, and perhaps a little overwhelming, even if 42 is the answer to life, the universe and everything. There may also be problems that you may be facing which this book doesn't specifically cover, but if you have this neat little toolkit, you can use it for problems unseen today or in the future.

_____

* Regretfully, my editor informs me that in 2021, they may have been the shoes of the summer – see https://www.independent.co.uk/life-style/fashion/crocs-nicki-minaj-christopher-kane-balenciaga-justin-bieber-b1845653.html.

Likewise, *The 7 Questions* have been expertly curated and will guide you on an inside-out, transformational journey that loosely follows the 'Four Worlds' German existential coaching model which addresses the relationship with yourself (*Eigenwelt*), others (*Mitwelt*), your beliefs (*Uberwelt*) and the environment around you (*Umwelt*). This helps provide structure and to give logical order to the questions.

THE PSYCHOLOGICAL REALM
Your Relationship with Yourself

The questions we will visit in this realm are:

How Did I Form My Opinion of Myself? (Chapter 1) – particularly useful for boosting self-esteem, especially after a job loss or break-up, or after enduring a difficult childhood or bullying.

Am I Lacking Any Fundamental Needs? (Chapter 2) – this is an essential question to ask that gets us to look at our inherent human needs, which, if met, will make us mentally and physically thrive like never before.

Am I Running From Anything? (Chapter 3) – a powerful question that is especially helpful for addressing any negative, self-sabotaging or addictive behaviours.

THE SOCIAL REALM
Your Relationships with Other People

What is My Hidden Motivation? (Chapter 4) – a fantastic question for exploring *why* you want to do anything, but it is also very important for looking at why we do the things we do in our relationships with others, as well as why we truly want to achieve some of our goals.

THE SPIRITUAL REALM
Your Life Purpose and Priorities

The questions we will cover in this realm are:

What's Most Important to Me? (Chapter 5) – this question can be used to resolve dilemmas, such as choosing a career path and discovering core values which can lead one to finding their life purpose.

Are My Beliefs Serving Me? (Chapter 6) – this deep and soul-searching question helps us to begin to identify, release and let go of beliefs that may no longer be serving us.

THE PHYSICAL REALM
Your Environment and the World Around You

What's the Next Smallest Step I Can Take? (Chapter 7) – this is a simple yet powerful question that empowers us to break through procrastination and to make positive changes in our lives as well as in the world around us.

The answers are often within

Part of my job as a life coach is giving advice, which can be a useful tool. For example: don't drink six double vodkas on a night out and then eat a kebab after! But if there was just one piece of advice I could give that would change your life, it would be this: **sleep more**. Adequate sleep is a fundamental human need and is essential for peak performance and mental health (as I'll explain later in Chapter 2). But in many situations, advice isn't what someone needs, nor is it useful. Giving advice can certainly be useful in coaching, and it has its place, particularly in the realm of sports and business coaching. But like every tool, there are limitations to what issues it can fix, and the problem is that most advice does not lead to further self-discovery.

Despite all of my experience and training, there is only one expert on your life: **you**. Nobody else has lived your life and experienced what you have. The answers to the reasons why you are stuck, why you procrastinate, why you have bad habits, why you keep repeating old patterns, and so forth, are often already within you. The issue is that these answers are hard to make conscious. And without more insight and conscious awareness, you will be very likely to repeat the same unconscious patterns for the rest of your life, running on autopilot. To quote the psychoanalyst Carl Jung: 'Until you make the unconscious conscious, it will direct your life, and you will call it fate.' But with the right questions, you can start to unearth those answers and patterns.

This is where I come in as your life coach: I will create a space for you to allow those important answers to surface from your subconscious, teasing them out with insightful questions, as I would in an actual life coaching session. While I'm not with you physically, I am here in spirit, offering my professional insight into the questions. *The 7 Questions* provides another level of thinking for you to reflect on.

How to use this book

By reading this book, you are now entering a life coaching session with me. The questions you'll read in this book are questions that I would ask my clients.

Whenever you come across a question, take a moment, even if it's just a few seconds, to reflect on the question asked, and then read the text that follows. You can, of course, go more in-depth and write down your answers instead of thinking about them – the choice is yours.

How should we work together?

As your coach, I would like you to:

- Read this book and with an open mind.
- Take the time you need to pause and reflect on the questions.
- Complete the suggested Growth Actions.

What about you? What would you like to achieve by reading this book? Perhaps you'd like to improve your self-confidence, understand why you do the things you do, or find your purpose in life. Take a moment to reflect on this before proceeding on to Chapter 1. Inside every single one of us is an unlimited source of potential for personal growth – and the way we will tap into this is through asking the right questions. Together, let's discover your truth and help you become the person you knew you always could be.

CHAPTER 1

How Did I Form My Opinion of Myself?

*'We're all born princes and the civilising process
turns us into frogs.'*

—ERIC BERNE

There was once a frog who thought he was ugly. Why? Because every time he looked at his reflection, he saw a contorted and uneven face, with murky brown spots all over it. He *hated* what he saw. All the other frogs were mean to him and ridiculed him for looking different – which only reinforced his feeling of ugliness. So, he decided to seek the help of a wise old wizard and asked him if he could make him handsome. 'Every time I look in the mirror, I just hate what I see!' cried the frog. The wizard agreed to help. But rather than casting a spell on him, he asked the frog if he could show him where he had seen his reflection. So, the frog took the old wizard to a puddle of water. As soon as he did, the old wizard smiled, and told the frog, 'If you look at a dirty puddle, you will always think you are dirty!' He then held up a pristine mirror to the young frog. And suddenly, for the first time in his life, the frog saw his reflection clearly, and he saw that he wasn't an ugly frog at all.

Quite the contrary – he was a very handsome prince! All this time, he *thought* he was an ugly frog, because of the beliefs he had created based on how others had treated him. It turned out that the frog had been looking in all the wrong places to find out who he was. In the end, he simply had to see more clearly to see the truth. Just as a painting doesn't know its own beauty, or a diamond isn't aware of its own worth, sometimes a prince (or princess) can struggle to realise their own royalty.

Our opinion of ourselves is fundamentally what determines our *self-esteem*. No baby is born into this world with a low opinion of their self; *low self-esteem* is a learned belief and behaviour. What is self-esteem? According to the *Cambridge English Dictionary*, it is 'belief and confidence in your own ability and value' and 'respect for yourself'. Another way to see self-esteem is how you feel about yourself: do you like, love or loathe yourself? Being low in self-esteem can make you prone to depression, addiction, social isolation, toxic relationships, jealousy and anger. A change in circumstances, such as loss of a job, a break-up or financial loss, could completely break you – as it did with me.

Our self-esteem is determined largely by seven key things:

1. Our core identity (who we think we are)
2. Our 'identity story' (how we think our past defines us)
3. How we view mistakes and imperfections
4. Whether we interpret negative events as 'our fault'
5. How we think we measure up to others
6. Our core beliefs
7. Our integrity

Do you often introduce yourself by what you *do*? Do you ever use the statement 'I am a' followed by a title, such as 'mother', 'father' or a job title? Do you beat yourself up for making mistakes? If so, it's possible that you haven't discovered who you really are – your *true identity*. Without discovering this, you are likely to have unstable or low self-esteem.

Knowing your true identity is really important and beneficial to building stable and higher self-esteem, which in turn means you will become more authentically confident and content in all aspects of your life, including in your career, your love life and your social life. Your earning potential can also increase with higher self-esteem, as shown by psychology research.* Furthermore, the more your self-esteem increases, the less abuse you are willing to tolerate from others and the more willing you are to walk away from toxic people and situations.

What you're about to read are true stories from my life as well as from my clients' lives. The very same things could happen to you – or worse – if you don't stop to discover your true identity *right now*. The way to find this out is to ask yourself, 'How did I form my opinion of myself?'

In this chapter, we are going to explore how to answer that question and find out how to build genuine self-esteem with some powerful questions.

First, we will look at separating who you are from what you do or have, as well as how well you do the things you do, or how you feel.

Then, we will explore the *identity story* of who you think you are – and why you might be severely mistaken. I will also present a very simple but powerful way you can feel better about a lot of past and current situations from your life.

We will also examine the risks of trying to be perfect, and how this can damage your self-esteem.

---

* Francesco Drago, 'Self-Esteem and Earnings'. IZA Discussion Paper No. 3577. Available at SSRN: https://ssrn.com/abstract=1158974 or http://dx.doi.org/10.1111/j.0042-7092.2007.00700.x.

The loss of jobs, relationships
and low self esteem

Never did I imagine myself at the age of twenty-five to be crying in the therapist's office. 'I used to be a successful up-and-coming CEO,' I sobbed. 'Who am I now? I'm *nobody*.'

Several years before I had co-founded the FDBK dating app,* I was running a different company, giftgaming, which had recently been valued at £1.7 million after a third round of investment. I was a *CEO* – that was my identity. I felt so much pride and power introducing myself and telling people what I did for a living. For four years, my business card said: 'Nick Hatter – Founder & CEO'.

I started the company after becoming disillusioned with my previous identity of being a computer programmer in a basement (literally) for an IT firm in the north of England. I remember being micromanaged, mocked by colleagues and feeling out of place and out of my depth compared to the geniuses I worked with – all top-performing computer science graduates from top universities who *lived and breathed* computer science (sometimes at the expense of personal hygiene or social awareness). This was evident when we would go to the pub after work, and they would often continue to discuss programming and software engineering, whereas I wanted to talk about *anything* but that!

Pretty soon, it became apparent that I didn't belong in this world. The job required me to work more than forty hours a week and, occasionally, to work oncall at the weekends, and sometimes I'd have to get up in the early hours to respond

---

* FDBK ('Feedback') is a dating app that gently gives you peer feedback data on your profile so that you can improve your chances of finding a match. It also rewards you for giving feedback to others – see: www.fdbk-app.com.

to IT emergencies. The managers' way of greeting me daily wasn't 'How are you doing?', or 'Hello', it was 'Do these tickets.' I'm pretty sure the computer servers got treated with more respect than me.

'*Is this it?*' I groaned to myself some days. It didn't help that the office had steel bars on the windows, which only compounded the prison-like feeling I was experiencing. I needed to break free. Something *had* to change. This is certainly how many of my life-coaching clients feel when they come to see me.

So, I decided I was going to start my own company. I began researching where to meet investors. Apparently, start-up weekends were the place to do it. I had missed the start-up weekend at the University of Southampton (my alma mater), so I decided I would sneak into the event at the University of Cambridge. Little did I know that this weekend would change my life. In just forty-eight hours, I had conceived a novel way of doing in-game advertising which would later become known as 'gift-gaming'. And thus, my identity would soon go from 'programmer in a basement' to 'Founder & CEO'. Nice.

A lot of in-game advertising at the time was a bit too tacky and involved creating custom-branded game items. For example, a branded virtual sword (with a soft drink brand like Coca-Cola) that gives you extra firepower. Other options were way too intrusive to the gaming experience, such as watching video ads to gain virtual game currency or extra lives. Giftgaming, however, would give the existing in-game currency or extra lives as a 'gift' to the player, courtesy of the brand. The virtual gifts would only take a few seconds to open, they didn't require custom-made items and would work for an infinite number of games and brands, so the idea was highly *scalable* (which in entrepreneurial speak meant it could have made *a lot* of money without having high overheads).

To my surprise, the University of Cambridge offered me a free place at the Cambridge Judge Business School as part of their start-up accelerator, Accelerate Cambridge, to pursue this idea. Seeing as they didn't want any equity or money from me, I took up their offer in a heartbeat. I quit my day job, sold everything I owned and relocated to Cambridge. Some days, I survived on just baked beans and orange juice – because that was all I could afford. During the week I would build my business, and, at the weekends, I would attend lectures and get entrepreneurial coaching at the business school.

Before I knew it, my start-up was being featured in tech news publications – including *TechCrunch*, *Management Today*, *Cambridge News* and *Business Weekly* – and I had floods of emails from investors. I was barely twenty-four years old, and I had raised £250,000 over three rounds of investment. I had some notable games companies signing up to my platform including King (maker of *Candy Crush*) and Square Enix (maker of the *Final Fantasy* series). For a while, giftgaming was even used in US rapper Fetty Wap's game, Nitro Nation Stories. I was also in talks with large soft drink companies, such as discussions with PepsiCo as to how we could get Mountain Dew advertised in video games in a cool new way. Things only seemed to look better and better for my humble little company. But, in March 2017, my life was to change again, only this time for the worse.

I ended up suffering a psychotic break that totally incapacitated me. I had panic attack after panic attack, and I became scared of trees and objects 'pointing at me'. Perhaps it was the long and hard hours I had put in, or the chronic lack of sleep and caffeine abuse. Maybe it was my repressed childhood trauma from growing up in a dysfunctional family and going to a very rough school. Or possibly a combination of all these things.

After six months, and much psychotherapy and psychiatric treatment, I was functional again, but my business was a smouldering crater. Clients and investors were chasing me for updates, but I didn't have it in me any more to run the company. I had had enough of the advertising world and the mobile games world.

Making money for the sake of it no longer appealed to me. I realised I wanted to do something more wholesome and meaningful. Some might perhaps call this *post-traumatic growth* – the personal transformation that comes after surviving a traumatic event.

So, I made the painful decision to step away from the company that I had spent over four years of my life building. I put the company into liquidation and gave the proceeds back to shareholders. And, just like that, I was no longer a CEO. My company went from being worth £1.7 million to *zero* – and so did my self-worth and my identity. I then had to go to the housing benefits office, cap in hand, and ask for help paying rent and bills, which was certainly one of the most humbling days of my life.

And that's how I ended up in the therapist's office, crying about how I was a *nobody*. After I had moved to London from Cambridge, I had days where I would cry and would be tempted to throw myself in front of an oncoming train on the London Underground – because I felt like a failure.

Finding a stable identity to overcome low self-esteem

Evidently, basing one's identity in a job, a business, a relationship or financial status is inherently *unstable*. What we need is a way to define ourselves that is not based on shaky ground, since loss and change are inevitable parts of life. This new foundation for self-identity needs to be based on stable factors that transcend anything external and fleeting. Our true identity is who we really are at the deepest possible level. It is unchanged by what we have (or don't have) or by how we feel (or don't feel).

Many of us define ourselves by external factors – such as our qualifications and what we do for a living, how much money we have, or whether we have a romantic partner, a six-pack, children or a published book. One of the most common questions we ask at social or networking events is: 'What do you *do*?'

People can easily become depressed when they lose one of these factors, especially their job, not only because of the loss of financial security, but because the prime factor that has given them their identity has been stripped away.

Identity loss can take various forms. A common problem I hear in my coaching practice, for example, is one experienced by mothers like Jeanine. Before her daughter was born, Jeanine was a high-flying lawyer. But now, instead of helping companies change their legal procedures, she was changing nappies: 'Before I had children, I was a career gal. A go-getter. But now I spend much of my time looking after my daughter. I feel like I'm just a mother. I don't know who I am any more. I feel like I could be so much more.'

The loss of a relationship can also be traumatic for self-identity. Robert, a successful writer, came to see me after he had been dumped by his girlfriend, which had put his self-esteem at an all-time low. I asked Robert how he would rate his self-esteem out of ten, to which he replied, 'about three'. Before, he was somebody's boyfriend. Now, he was single – which he equated with 'being a failure'.

Even being successful in business is not enough to mask the pain of low self-esteem. Brad, a seasoned and successful tech entrepreneur, had it all: a net worth of over £10 million, and a few nice houses and supercars. Initially, Brad came to see me to improve his work productivity.

However, we later discovered through deeper coaching that, as a competitive achiever, he would need to achieve more and more to feel better: 'I've got to have the best of everything. So that means having the very best supercars and the best watches.'

I asked Brad, 'At what point will you have enough money, cars and watches?' To which he replied, 'I see your point.'

As we can see from Brad's case, nothing *external* can fill the internal void of low self-esteem or a poor self-identity. And even if it does, it is very short-lived. When we use achievements to make ourselves feel good, we need another achievement to feel good again. If we use qualifications, then we need another qualification. And so forth for possessions, money or anything extrinsic.

So how do you define yourself? What have you learned by asking yourself this question? Does your identity depend heavily on extrinsic attributes?

The who-what-how model

Let's separate who you are into three key components using the Who-What-How (WWH) model:

1. **Who?** *Who* are you being? This is talking about *character* and refers to intrinsic qualities, for example: confident, generous, caring, intelligent, and so forth. This is the part of self that is truly important and what your true friends and romantic partners like about you. It's what they will say about you at your funeral.

   You can be super-rich or accomplished, but if you're not of good character, I can guarantee you will not have many friends (except false ones who want to be around you in the hope of somehow benefiting from your money, status or success).

2. **What?** *What* do you have or do? This refers to *possessions*, *vocation* and *relationships*. This could be what you do for work, or whether you have a partner, kids or good looks. While your loved ones and real friends may mention your good works at your funeral, the reason they will mourn you will be because of *who* you were, not because of what you *had* or *did*. Your actions were simply a by-product of *who* you were.

3. **How?** *How* do you do what you do? *How* do you feel? This can be how well or how poorly you perform a task, or how well (or not well) you embody a certain character trait. Your fans, colleagues and maybe your bosses at your funeral may miss that you did your job well. Certainly, when I heard Chris Cornell of the hard rock band, Soundgarden, had passed away, I was sad – he was a great musician and singer. The same with Chester Bennington of the alt-rock band, Linkin Park. But I didn't know *who* they were personally, only *how* well they performed.

It's important to not confuse *how* well you do or did something with *who* you are. Some celebrities are amazing at *how* well they do what they do, but that doesn't necessarily mean they are likeable for *who* they are.

Some successful politicians and leaders are hated by many; Hollywood film producers and billionaire moguls have been convicted of sexual abuse and harassment; glamorous supermodels and actors have verbally and physically abused their assistants and on-set staff. Some wildly successful artists have also battled low self-esteem and depression.

As seen with these examples, job title, wealth, fame or success is not necessarily correlated with likeability, character or self-esteem. But yet, the mistake that many people make is that, deep down, they want to be successful so that they feel worthy and lovable. It's such a shame that many people strive to be successful, but how many strive to be of good *character*?

One of my coachees, James, was a successful psychiatrist – maybe even *too* successful. He had run his private London psychiatry practice for over fifteen years and lived a comfortable life with his family in Holland Park. His partner, however, felt neglected and bitter as a result, and even said, 'I wish you had never bloody started your private practice in the first place!' So much for success making you more lovable. Furthermore, even though James had many qualifications and a very successful business, he suffered from low self-esteem. One question I asked him during a coaching session was, 'Who are you without your achievements?' He paused for a long time before he said, 'I really don't know.'

So, I told James, 'Go and ask your friends why they're friends with you. If they're only friends with you because you're successful, ditch them, because they're not real friends. But more likely than not, they will tell you what they like about you and who you show up as to them.'

Next week, he came back to me and listed a bunch of characteristics, such as *intelligent, thoughtful* and *interesting*. While this didn't solve all of James's self-esteem issues, it was a step in the right direction; it helped him explore himself beyond his work – which, in the past, he had based much of his worth and identity on and he couldn't get enough accomplished to feel good about himself.

Perhaps the WWH model seems simple and obvious. But it's amazing how many of us forget to separate ourselves from what we do, what we have, how well we do our job or how we feel. Think of the people whose self-esteem has absolutely crashed after losing a job (as mine did) or a relationship. Sometimes we can over-identify with how we feel. For example, we say 'I *am* sad' rather than 'I *feel* sad'. Put your feelings in the *How* section of the WWH model. Your feelings can change, but does your core character change? Some days you may feel sad, but does this mean sadness has to be part of your true identity? Of course not. In fact, many meditative practices involve simply detaching and observing your feelings. In doing so, we can start to experience relief from the ups and downs of our emotions and become the observer.

In Acceptance and Commitment Therapy (ACT) based coaching, there's a process called 'cognitive defusion' which is very similar to meditation; it also involves detaching from your thoughts and feelings, perhaps seeing them like leaves on a stream. Again, this can provide relief from negative emotions. And, in using the WWH model, you too can experience relief: you are not your feelings – these belong in the *How* section of the model.

What about mental illness? You can have depression, but do you have to *be* depressed – does it have to be part of your true identity? Not according to the WWH model, because mental illness is something you *have*. It can also be a feeling, in which case, it belongs in the *How*, not in the *Who* section.

There was a woman who, upon meeting her therapist for the first time, stretched out her hand and said, 'Hi, I'm bipolar.' Her therapist smiled and shook her hand, saying, 'Hi, I'm Mark.' Some people can define themselves by their illnesses. For example, we sometimes see people including their mental health diagnoses, such as bipolarity, in their bio on social media, as if it's part of their identity.

While there is absolutely no shame in having a mental illness, it really doesn't have to define *who* you are, any more than having a physical illness does. Can you imagine if people started posting their physical illnesses on Twitter and over-identifying with them? '*Nick Hatter. Life Coach. Chronic runny nose. Asthma guy*'.

As someone in addiction recovery for over five years, I bristle a little bit every time I hear someone say, 'My name is X and I'm an addict.' What kind of connotations come up with that word, 'addict'? To me, they're pretty negative: someone who is irresponsible, out of control, selfish and lowly regarded in society. Sure, it is important to admit you have a problem, but it's also important to not let that problem *define* you. If you do define yourself by your problem, you are more likely to reinforce that behaviour.

It was, in fact, my first life coach, Hans Schumann, who

called me out on this very behaviour. I remember saying to him in a life coaching session, 'I'm a work and food addict.' And he firmly challenged me on the implications of me labelling myself like this. Initially, I was very defensive – it's what I had defined myself as for several years! Who the hell was he to take this away from me? However, with time, I came to accept that this didn't have to be my core identity; my addictions didn't have to define me.

Hans warned me that by labelling myself as an addict, I was more likely to do addictive behaviours – because that's who I am after all, right? Wrong. Labelling Theory in psychology is the idea that one's self-identity can become a self-fulfilling prophecy. Sociology professors Teresa Scheid and Eric Wright summarise the issue well on the subject of mental health:

> One begins to self-identify as [a] mentally ill person. And because this identity becomes 'who I am', patients with [a] disorder expect themselves to be ill and continue to exhibit symptoms ... Because he or she has internalised and identified with the mental patient role. In short, people who are labelled as deviant and treated as deviant become deviant. Mental illness becomes the issue around which one's identity and life become organised – a 'deviant career'.*

If you have a mental health condition, my heart goes out to you, truly and sincerely. I know what it's like to have anxiety, depression and post-traumatic stress disorder – all three have crippled me at several points in my life. But if people start to treat you differently because of your mental health label, then as per Scheid's and Wright's summary, this may become

---

* T. Scheid and E. Wright, *A Handbook for the Study of Mental Health* (3rd edition, 2017), 140.

a self-fulfilling prophecy and prevent you from becoming better. By over-identifying with mental health labels, you may start telling yourself, 'I can't change – *this is who I am*' which could impede any progress at recovery or personal growth.

Remember, you are *so* much more than some mental health label. When I was at a trauma retreat, one psychotherapist said to me: 'These mental health labels were only meant to be used by the *professionals* – not the patients. A lot of harm has been done because of patients using them.'

Of course, I might have a job as a life coach, but *who* I am as a person is so much more. If you ask my friends, they will (hopefully) tell you that I'm funny, interesting, intelligent, sensitive, caring and generous. As a spiritual person, I would also say I am an imperfect child of God/the Universe/a Higher Power (whatever you want to call it). This is unchanging and no situation or circumstance can *ever* take that away from me – unlike a CEO title!

Take a moment to reflect on your own *who*, *what* and *how*. If you have applied the WWH model to yourself, then regardless of what you have, or what you do, or how you feel, your core character remains unchanging. This gives you a solid foundation for defining yourself and knowing who you truly are in a world that is constantly changing.

We have explored self-identity in terms of separating character, vocation, possessions, success, wealth, labels and skill. But another crucial component to discovering who you really are is the *story* that you tell yourself about past events.

GROWTH ACTION

Self identity discovery

1. Ask your closest three friends (or colleagues):

    i) Why are you friends with me? What do you
       like about me?
    ii) What is the one thing I could do to improve
        as a friend or human being?

Write down a list of what they say and keep it.

2. Using the Who-What-How model, write down
   these qualities in the Who section and know
   that this is who you are showing up as in the
   world today.

How has your identity changed as a result of doing
this exercise?

Change your story, change your life

We all have an *identity story* of who we think we are. This story
is often based on what has happened to us in the past and how
others have treated us. These identity stories can be quite
subtle and insidious; they are formed over many years and
events. Eventually, they become an automatic narrative that
we tell ourselves about who we are, for example, 'I must not
be good enough' or 'There's something wrong with me'. The
problem is that some stories are incredibly disempowering and
can result in low self-esteem. Thus, if we can change the story
we created from those events, we can very quickly improve our

self-esteem. What if I told you that you weren't to blame? What if I told you that there was *nothing* wrong with you, and that the people around you were sick, dysfunctional or abusive, or had other things going on for them that had nothing to do with you?

Your story may not be true

If I'm totally honest, I would say I *loathed* myself for many years. The story I had made up was that I was just simply not good enough as a human being. I had several points of reference to back this up with, after all. I felt my older brothers were mean to me at times and I was quite unpopular at school, college and even at university, and I seemed to have quite a few unrequited loves in my life.

When I was around fourteen years old, I asked out a girl at school, Valerie. Like me, she was good at science, and we were both in the top set. Perhaps she'd be good girlfriend material for an intellectual like me? Unfortunately, when I asked her out in front of her friends she said 'no'. Then her friends laughed. I went home that day feeling pretty worthless, and a story was formed in my mind: 'She said no because I'm not good or attract-ive enough.' This would later become part of my identity story: 'I'm not good or attractive enough.'

Over twelve years later, I reconnected with Valerie. She's happily married now with two kids.

As we were catching up, Valerie said something that would completely blow me away and make me question my iden-tity story.

'Nick, do you remember when you asked out all the girls in our year?' she teasingly asked.

'Oh, man. That was an embarrassing phase of my life! And I asked you out too!' I replied.

'Yes, you did.'

'Oh yes I remember now – and you said "no"!' I blushed.

'Well ... here's the thing ... that day you asked me out ... I wanted to say yes – *really* badly! And I couldn't because I was too scared of what my friends would think. And that day, I was so upset that when I got home, I cried!'

I was absolutely shocked when she said this.

'Wait a second! You mean to tell me that for *twelve years*, I thought you had rejected me because there was something wrong with *me*?'

'Yes!' she laughed.

I couldn't believe it. All this time, I had assumed I was the problem. That I was simply not good enough and not handsome enough. *Where else had I created a story like this and was wrong?*

This reminds me of one of my clients, Anja, who was a celebrity dancer; attractive, very successful, and with loads of social media followers. She had been on TV a lot and was interviewed by the press many times. But Anja was going through a break-up – and, like many relationship break-ups, her self-esteem was taking a massive hit, because the story she had made up was that she was to blame and that she wasn't good enough.

While she wasn't clinically depressed, Anja definitely had days where she just wanted to binge-eat and stay in bed all day. Her career could have been doing better and her agent was starting to get a bit concerned about her. I suspect had I not intervened when I did, she could well have ended up needing more clinical or even psychiatric help.

I did a very simple exercise with her: I drew a horizontal line with a vertical line intersecting it on a Post-it note and asked her, 'What does this mean?'

She squinted and then said, 'It's a cross.'

'What else could it be?' I asked.

'Perhaps it's a chart?'

'And what else?'

'Oh, I know! It's a two-by-two matrix!'

'And what else?'

'Um, a crossroad?'

All by herself, she had managed to come up with several different interpretations.

'You see, human beings are meaning-making machines,' I explained to her. 'You've looked at the same symbol but notice how you're able to come up with a number of different interpretations.'

Then I asked her, 'You seemed pretty sure about your first interpretation. Given that there are numerous possible interpretations and meanings, how do you know for sure which interpretation is the correct one?'

'Well ... I don't,' she replied.

'That's right – because unless I tell you what I meant, or unless you have more data, you can't say for sure. I drew this symbol, but only I can tell you what I meant.'

I then asked her to look at the symbol again.

'This time, I want you to look at this symbol, but I want you to imagine it's your break-up we are looking at, and I want you to do the *exact* same process we just did – you seem to be good at finding different interpretations.'

'Well ... my first interpretation is that it's all my fault. I made many mistakes in the relationship. I could have treated him better.'

'And what other interpretations could there be?'

'I'm not sure.'

'Well, what other explanations could there be for him wanting to end the relationship?'

Anja thought for a moment, and then replied, 'Maybe he's going through some of his own stuff right now?'

'Yes, he could well be. What else?'

'Hmm ... Maybe he's not a compatible partner?'

'You're doing great Anja!'

'That's interesting, I never saw it like this before.'

The map is not the territory

Suddenly, it seemed like Anja had a light bulb moment. Her face lit up. Something had shifted. I could have told her the answer, but it's much more powerful when the client comes to the realisation themselves. All I did was introduce Anja to the neurolinguistic programming (NLP) presupposition of 'the map is not the territory'.

NLP is a psychological framework that examines how thoughts (neuro), language (linguistic) and behaviour (programming) interact with each other.* It can provide practical ways to change the way that we think, view past events and our perspective on our life, such as by *presuppositions*, which are convenient assumptions or beliefs that are generally helpful for both professionals and clients to assume. In Anja's case, it was life-changing.

According to NLP, we often respond to our subjective *map* (perception) of the *terrain* (life), of people and events, rather than actual reality. It's a bit like looking at a map that says there's a lake in the terrain, but when you look at the terrain itself, you realise there is no lake – *the map itself is wrong*. Our beliefs in life can be exactly like that incorrect map – just like I was wrong about why I thought Valerie had rejected me. And the same can go for our identity and who we think we are.

Using the interpretations exercise with the 'cross' symbol, Anja was able to find a new interpretation for her break-up – one that was more optimistic and less self-blaming.

As I tell my coachees: *one of the best ways to improve your*

---

* While some question its evidence basis, NLP has been widely used by many therapists, coaches and psychologists. Several NLP techniques and models have also evolved into various proven trauma and phobia treatments such as EMDR (Eye Movement Desensitisation and Reprocessing) and the 'rewind' technique. See https://www.nlpco.com/library/eye-movement-integration-therapy/ and https://www.hgi.org.uk/useful-information/treatment-dealing-ptsd-trauma-phobias/rewind-technique.

self-esteem is to stop blaming yourself for other people's crappy behaviour.

When I checked in with Anja several months later, she had found a new boyfriend and she also said that she was able to use the same exercise for challenging her jealous feelings in her new relationship. She had kept the original Post-it note I gave her as a reminder to ask herself: *What other interpretations are there?*

Every time she felt jealous or hurt, she could calm herself down and ask herself this question first before getting overly reactive and angry. The great thing about life coaching is that when you touch one person's life, it can have a ripple effect and touch other people's lives too and, soon, you're sending out a ripple of positive change into the world.

If you have been bullied at school or work, or had abusive parents, colleagues or partners, you may well suffer from low self-esteem – because your *interpretation* of those past events leads you to believe that *you* are the problem. Growing up, my family hurt me in many ways, both physically and emotionally. And children often don't blame their parents or relatives; they blame *themselves* – just like I did with Valerie and Anja with her ex-boyfriend. One secret to raising self-esteem is thus to stop blaming yourself for others' abusive behaviour.

Hurt people *hurt* people – it's probably not your fault

When I worked as a programmer, I was mistreated by a few colleagues as well as managers. Like many bullied people, I started to blame myself for the way they were treating me – again the story was: 'It's *my* fault – I must be unlikeable or bad at my job.' Looking back now, I can see that it was they who were sick and hurt. And hurt people *hurt* people; bullies themselves have low self-esteem and feel disempowered, and they try to make themselves feel better by belittling others.

There was nothing wrong with me – it just was a sick

environment, and the wrong culture for my personality. Unfortunately, there are a lot of people in life who are mentally or spiritually sick in one way or another. Virginia Satir, one of the renowned psychotherapists NLP was modelled after and the godmother of family therapy, estimates 96 per cent of families in the US alone are dysfunctional, having studied 10,000 of them herself.* By dysfunctional, she meant engaging in a number of unhealthy behaviours, such as abuse, addiction or co-dependency (trying to fix someone).

I dare say with our repressive, self-deprecating, somewhat cynical and alcoholic culture, as well as the fact that we have some of the unhappiest children in the world, the percentage of dysfunctional families is probably about the same for the UK.† According to researchers, nearly a third of our society can be classified as 'binge drinkers', based on how much they can drink!‡

Dysfunctional families create dysfunctional people, so it's important not to blame yourself when others mistreat you. As the philosopher Jiddu Krishnamurti said, 'It is no measure of health to be well adjusted to a profoundly sick society.' Remember, our 'society' was once the same society that decided, by consensus at one point, that:

- Slavery was necessary and acceptable
- Women were not reliable witnesses in court and were not deemed worthy of being allowed to vote in elections

---

* 'The New Face of Codependency' – https://www.addictioninfamily.com/family-issues/new-face-of-codependency/ – accessed 7 May 2020.
† The Children's Society, *The Good Childhood Report*, 2015. http://www.childrenssociety.org.uk/sites/default/files/TheGoodChildhoodReport2015.pdf.
‡ Office for National Statistics, Adult drinking habits in Great Britain, 2018. https://www.ons.gov.uk/peoplepopulationandcommunity/healthandsocialcare/drugusealcoholandsmoking/datasets/adultdrinkinghabits – accessed 21 March 2021.

- Watching people being eaten alive by lions was
  'entertainment' (known as *damnatio ad bestias* during
  Roman times)

That's a lot of sickness and dysfunction! What is acceptable today may, fifty or a hundred years from now, make us cringe and ask, 'What on earth were we thinking?' And yet, we still seem to blame ourselves when people mistreat, abuse, shame or mock us, or if we don't get selected for that job or role.

In positive psychology, there's a concept known as 'explanatory style', which is how you explain events and circumstances to yourself. In both mine and Anja's cases, we had a *pessimistic* explanatory style – we believed that the cause of these events was entirely *internal*, that we were the cause. Optimistic people, however, attribute events and circumstances to *external* causes, i.e. things outside of themselves. Research by psychologists such as Dr Martin Seligman shows that someone who tends to blame themselves for negative events tends to exhibit lower self-esteem, more depression, lower immune function and even higher morbidity than someone who attributes failure to external causes.*† If we had an X-ray scanner for other people's emotional baggage and wounds, we probably wouldn't blame ourselves as often!

I have certainly had consultations before with people who had had a series of misfortunes and believed that they had somehow 'manifested' those negative events into existence with their negative thinking or energy. So not only were they suffering misfortunes, but they were also actively blaming themselves

---

* S. F. Maier and M. E. Seligman, 'Learned helplessness: Theory and evidence', *Journal of Experimental Psychology: General*, 105:1 (1976), 3–46. https://doi.org/10.1037/0096-3445.105.1.3.
† C. Peterson, M. E. Seligman and G. E. Vaillant, 'Pessimistic explanatory style is a risk factor for physical illness: A thirty-five-year longitudinal study', *Journal of Personality and Social Psychology*, 55:1 (1988), 23–27. https://doi.org/10.1037/0022-3514.55.1.23.

because they believed they had created the events – this certainly doesn't help! Thus, a pessimistic explanatory style is potentially damaging for mental and physical health, as proven by psychology research. Instead, a more optimistic way to look at life is to remember that sometimes bad things happen that are completely outside of our control – regardless of whether we 'think positive thoughts'.

The cycle of low self-esteem

Low self-esteem is an *unconscious negative bias* against ourselves. In other words, it will cause us to unconsciously pick the worst possible interpretations of negative events where we come out as a bad or defective person. The low self-esteem cycle is as follows:

- 'There's something wrong with me'
  (Initial toxic belief created from negative events)
- 'Therefore, this bad event or outcome is my fault'
  (Unconscious bias against self because of toxic belief)
- 'Therefore, there's something wrong with me'
  (Toxic belief reinforced)

Thus, *all* negative events can start to reinforce that initial toxic and unhelpful belief that we are not good enough – if we let them. We need to keep asking ourselves, 'How did I form my opinion of myself?', as well as 'What other interpretations are there that do not involve me?', when a negative event makes us feel that we are bad and unworthy. You need to, in a way, become less self-centred and recognise that not everything negative is about you; you must stop being overly responsible for negative outcomes (where appropriate).

Making mountains out of molehills
(global v. local thinking)

It should also be noted that people with low self-esteem will
take a negative event and 'globalise' it. In other words, they will
judge their whole career, life or their identity off one bad event,
thinking, *This one bad event or outcome proves just how bad I am
in my career, my love life, and, in fact, just shows how inherently
defective I am!* A person with high self-esteem, however, will
'localise' a negative event or outcome: they will not use it to
make broad assessments on themselves and will instead keep
the negative outcome to its rightful domain. For example, a
salesperson with high self-esteem who gets a rejection from
a potential customer will not conclude, *That's it, I'm a lousy
salesperson, I'm also a terrible romantic partner and a person;
I'm basically useless.* Instead, they will think, *Even though I'm
disappointed, it was probably just that one customer.* Even if they
do have a string of rejections, rather than blame themselves,
the salesperson with high self-esteem will most likely blame
the general market conditions, or perhaps the product they are
selling, rather than themselves.

Positive events can reinforce low self-esteem

Even positive events have the potential to reinforce low
self-esteem:

- 'There's something wrong with me'
  (Initial unconscious negative bias against yourself)
- 'I only succeeded in this because I got lucky, or
  because they were just being nice, or another
  external factor'
  (Unconscious bias against self because of toxic belief)

- 'Therefore, I'm still probably not good enough'
  (Toxic belief reinforced)

This cycle can create 'Imposter Syndrome'* – the feeling of being an imposter. For example, when Dr Kate Brierton, a doctor of clinical psychology, left me a stellar review, saying that engaging me as her life coach was 'one of the best decisions she ever made', my unconscious negative bias against myself (the low self-esteem part of me) said, 'She didn't *really* mean it. She was just being nice!' I did notice, however, I said a similar thing for the other fifty-plus five-star reviews clients have left for me ...

For *positive* events, you'll want to respond in the opposite way to negative events: ask yourself, 'What did I do to contribute to this positive outcome?' If the answer is 'nothing' or 'I just got lucky', then you're most likely being afflicted by emotional black-and-white thinking – a type of 'cognitive distortion' (psychology's way of saying 'screwed-up thinking'). This happens when the amygdala (the security centre of the brain) puts us into a fight, flight, freeze or fawn (submissive) response. This process disconnects us from the pre-frontal cortex (the 'thinking', rational part of our brain), so we act irrationally or even stupidly, and we might end up doing things we later regret, once our 'thinking brain' kicks back in. This can be a useful survival mechanism, because if a tiger or a masked gunman suddenly enters the room, your brain needs to very quickly make snap decisions to save your life. But in a lot of cases, it's an inappropriate, irrational or unhelpful response. One way to break out of cognitive distortions is to simply be aware that you're being gripped by one. Another is to calm yourself down, which you can do with deep breathing and guided relaxation (such as through self-hypnosis – more on this in Chapter 7).

---

* It's technically 'Imposter Phenomenon' as one trainer taught me, because 'syndrome' implies it's a chronic disease, which it's not!

When we are emotionally aroused, we become, to put it simply, more stupid. So, we must calm ourselves down to think more clearly at times.

Healthy self-esteem is balanced

Of course, as with most healthy well-adjusted adults, the key is *balance*. Another NLP presupposition is 'responsibility leads to empowerment'. Indeed, taking responsibility for changing our lives and our mindset is crucial for bringing about change, lest we develop 'learned helplessness', where we believe that nothing we do will make a difference and that we are stuck where we are for ever. But yet, as we see with psychology research, and in Anja's case, taking excessive responsibility, especially for negative events, is very disempowering and can make us become a victim. People who live with addicts and try to fix them (co-dependents) certainly can suffer from this; they take too much responsibility for other people's actions. Survivors of bullying and abuse can also feel like it's their fault, and that they are somehow shameful or defective.

On the other hand, if we absolve ourselves completely of responsibility and blame everyone else in our lives (which is more typical of narcissists who have *too much* self-esteem), then this may lead us to believe we have no power at all to change our lives, which is equally disempowering. The opposite of crazy is still crazy.

Rejection is *always* subjective

Something my previous editor, Julia Kellaway, said to me: 'Just because a publisher or agent doesn't see the potential, it doesn't mean that your writing isn't good! It's entirely subjective.' Indeed, she's right – *someone's subjective opinion is not objective*:

- Just because they're not attracted to you, it doesn't mean you're not attractive.
- Just because they don't like your work, it doesn't mean you don't have talent.
- Just because they didn't pick you, it doesn't mean you're bad.

Think about The Beatles, who were told by Decca Recording, 'We don't like their sound; they have no future in showbiz.' The Beatles, of course, went on to become one of the most commercially successful bands of all time. Likewise, just because someone isn't attracted to you, or doesn't think you're good enough for that job or part, it doesn't mean that it's *objectively* true, nor is it representative of everyone else's opinion. There are certainly celebrities I don't find attractive who my friends do, and vice versa. I also love Marmite and Vegemite, but some think it's disgusting (their loss!).

If we think about it, lots of things are subjective. Let's take qualifications, for example; you are only qualified if a committee or a group of lecturers believes you have sufficiently understood or practise the subject matter to a certain level. Even scientific research papers are subjective to an extent; they are only deemed publishable once they have been peer-reviewed. Certain peers (who are deemed competent by other peers) then have to unanimously agree that the paper is scientifically sound and accurate. Likewise, in court, though the judge and jury try to be rational and logical, there is still an element of subjectivity when looking at legal arguments and evidence. For example, we see higher-level courts overturning decisions made by courts at lower levels all the time. The bottom line? Humans are subjective and emotional creatures, and thus, so too will be the 'objective' systems that we use to measure others, to some extent. Therefore, *even objectivity can be inherently subjective,* and you should keep this in mind before blaming yourself.

We have covered how interpreting events differently can change your identity story and as a result improve your self-esteem. Another facet we need to explore, though, for discovering how you form the opinion of yourself is your relationship to (im)perfection.

GROWTH ACTION

Self identity discovery

1. Consider the symbol below:

X

   i) What's your first interpretation of the above?

  ii) What other interpretations are there? How many can you come up with?

2. Now think of an event from your life where you created a story about who you thought you were. Perhaps it was an event where you felt like a bad person, out of place, or not good enough.

   i) What other interpretations could there be that do not involve you? What could have been going on for the other people? Take some time to consider how else the event could be interpreted.

  ii) How has your identity story changed as a result of doing this exercise?

You are imperfect – and that's OK

One cold winter's evening, I was on the floor, crying down the phone to my mum. A few things had happened: first, my finances were struggling somewhat – I had a significant and unexpected drop in my coaching revenue one month, and then one of my relatives defaulted on a loan I gave him which he promised he would repay (note: never lend more than you can afford to lose).

In addition, I had been messaging a lovely Irish woman on a dating app. Susie was a really attractive brunette – smart, spiritual and funny. We had one 45-minute phone conversation, and I thought it had gone very well. I was absolutely buzzing, and I couldn't wait to speak to her again.

But, to my horror, the next day she messaged me to say she didn't want to continue speaking with me. Apparently, I had talked mostly about myself, barely asked her any questions, and I had bragged about how much I got paid per hour as well as how many matches I had on the dating app. I felt like a complete idiot. Why did I do that?!

I begged Susie to give me another chance. I explained how the reason I had shown off was because, on reflection, I had been intimidated by her beauty and felt I needed to somehow prove myself as worthy of dating her (a lot of men fall into this trap). She said she appreciated my honesty and that she'd think about it and get back to me. However, unfortunately, she decided she still didn't want to speak to me and wished me the best of luck with dating. And that was the last I heard from Susie.

I felt crushed. Despite doing over thirteen years of personal development; despite the years of work I had done on myself in therapy, coaching, addiction recovery; despite all the books I'd read, I *still* managed to screw this up. I was furious with myself.

It hurt even more because I realised that, as a life coach, I felt that I needed to live a good example. Usually, I'd be helping clients with their love lives or improving their prosperity. And yet here I was, crying down the phone to my mum, telling her I felt like a failure because of my financial and romantic mistakes. Feeling completely worthless, I called another fellow in recovery for some moral support and, while we were talking, I found myself thinking about the basketball legend Michael Jordan.

Practice does *not* make perfect

Jordan is one of the top basketball players of all time and the world's richest athlete as of 2020.* To get to the six-time NBA champion's level of excellence and success, you would have to practise, practise and practise. And yet, despite his fantastic basketball abilities, Jordan admits that he missed more than nine thousand shots and lost almost three hundred games in his career. Furthermore, he says that twenty-six times he's been trusted to take the winning shot – and missed.†

So, Jordan is certainly not a *perfect* basketball player. My thinking was, therefore, that if Jordan, being one the world's best at what he does and having practised for hours and hours each day, is *still* able to make mistakes even while being at the top of his game, then maybe I can forgive myself for being less than perfect despite all of my training and personal development. And maybe you can too.

And at that moment, an epiphany came to me like a divine lightning bolt: *The reason I felt so horrible was because I expected myself to be perfect.*

Perfectionism is a learned behaviour that can develop over time. We can develop the belief that as long as we are perfect, then we are lovable. This might be because of people who criticised us when we inevitably made mistakes as children, such as hot-tempered or overly critical parents, relatives and teachers.

---

* https://www.forbes.com/profile/michael-jordan/ – accessed 2 May 2020.
† https://www.forbes.com/quotes/11194/ – accessed 9 May 2020.

Unfortunately, perfection is unattainable and thus such beliefs are often unhelpful and a barrier to healthy self-esteem. It's akin to living your life in a fragile glass bubble; it only takes a small chip or dent (i.e. any form of criticism) for your reality to completely shatter.

Many of us strive for perfection. Some of us may even feel inferior or defective if we are not perfect, or if we make mistakes. Sometimes we may even feel worthless and useless at times because of our imperfections, just like I did.

Imperfection still has value

It's strange how we can have a perfectionistic black-and-white way of thinking of ourselves: just because we might have flaws, or make mistakes, we might attribute ourselves as worthless. If you found a £20 note on the floor, even if it was crinkled, ripped and dirty, it would *still* be worth £20. How unfortunate and cap-italistic it is that we find it much easier and logical to attribute some value to material items, but not ourselves. Surely a human life is worth much more than a £20 note?

Your mistakes and your biggest character defects may well one day be worth a fortune when helping someone else. During my training as a coach, I heard a story about a marriage counsel-lor who was challenged by one of her clients who asked, 'Are you married?' The counsellor replied, 'No – in fact, I'm divorced.' Her client then asked, 'So what makes you qualified to give me advice then?' to which the counsellor replied, 'Well, I can certainly tell you what a *bad* marriage looks like.'

Any mistakes you make today can be recycled into valuable lessons that you or others can learn from later. This is certainly how many entrepreneurs view their past mistakes and failures in business. I learned from giftgaming that I can't do it all alone and that self-care is essential for long-term success.

In NLP, there is a presupposition: 'there is no such thing as failure, only feedback'. Children learn to walk through feedback, which only comes by making mistakes, by falling down and getting up again. Yet, how often are we our own harshest critics when we make a mistake?

Think about when you're learning something new, such as a song on a musical instrument. Most likely you will make several mistakes to begin with: you might hit the wrong notes or play out of time. But when you make the mistake, you correct it. And then what you're playing sounds even better. And the process continues until you have mastered the song. The same goes for mastering your life, your career and your relationships.

We can define ourselves by our failures or setbacks. However, failures can lead to great success. Here are a few famous examples:

- Thomas Edison took over a thousand attempts to successfully invent the light bulb.
- Author J. K. Rowling was rejected by over twenty publishers for *Harry Potter*.
- The oil lubricant WD40 allegedly took forty attempts to get the formula right, which is where its name is derived from.
- Oprah Winfrey was fired from her job as a TV presenter and this led to her founding her own media empire.
- Walt Disney was fired from a newspaper for 'having no original ideas'.
- Film director Steven Spielberg was rejected from the University of Southern California's film school three times.

But a setback is a set-up for a comeback; I've experienced many 'failures' in my own life, but now live a terrific life in the Canary Islands, I'm a successful life coach, a published author and the co-founder of a very promising dating app company. You too can be the hero of your story. To quote the writer C. S. Lewis (author of *The Chronicles of Narnia*): 'You can't go back and change the beginning, but you can start where you are and change the ending.'

In any case, all of us are learning to walk in life. Nobody is born with a perfect instruction manual. If a child fell down learning to walk, would you comfort them and encourage them to try again? Or would you berate and shame them for making a mistake and not being good enough?

We can often be our own worst enemy. We sometimes speak to ourselves in the most degrading and harsh manner possible. As a result, we may become perfectionists or workaholics, develop low self-esteem, or lack adequate self-care. We would all probably benefit from greater self-compassion and patience.

So how might a best friend or a loving parent treat you? How much kinder might you be to yourself? Most of us wouldn't dream of talking to a friend or a child the way we do to ourselves. So, it's time to let go of trying to be perfect. Do your best in life, but also forgive yourself when you inevitably make a mistake.

GROWTH ACTION

Let go of perfection

Challenge perfectionism

1. Wear odd socks for a week. Get comfortable with being imperfect!
2. Make a list of your flaws, then tell at least three family members or friends about them. Then ask them if they still like you.

3. Take up a new hobby and allow yourself to be awful
    at it. For example, learn a musical instrument, or try
    drawing something.
4. Now reflect on your life – where might mishaps
    and mistakes have led to more growth, learning and
    success overall? How would your life improve if you
    became more self-forgiving and self-compassionate?
5. How can you start being more self-forgiving?

Check your comparisons are fair

Sometimes, comparison can be a source of low self-esteem. If you're going to compare, make sure it's a *fair* comparison. For example, in the gym, it's easy to compare yourself to that ripped person in the changing rooms. However, there's no way to tell, just from looking at them, if they appear to be in better shape than you because they are using steroids, or maybe they are bulimic, or perhaps they have an exercise addiction.

How many times do we forget to ask ourselves if we are making a fair comparison? How do you know that your neighbour (you know the one, with the nicer car and house) isn't hiding a load of debt and are perhaps, in fact, on the verge of financial collapse? Even if they are wealthy, how do you know for sure that they haven't acquired that wealth through questionable means? Or perhaps they had a wealthy family who were able to give them ample financial support. Again, not every wealthy person is corrupt nor does every successful person come from a wealthy background. However, it's important to remember to ask yourself:

- Is this a fair comparison?

- Am I comparing my chapter 1 to their chapter 20?
- Am I comparing my insides to their outsides?

On a final note of comparison, I discovered one of the reasons why I get envious: it's because I think there isn't enough love to go around. But that's silly – because it's like asking if I love Soundgarden or Audioslave more (they're both great and both have had Chris Cornell as the lead singer). Or *Man's Search for Meaning* by Viktor Frankl or *The Road Less Travelled* by M. Scott Peck; both are different but great in their own right and have had a profound impact on me. Therefore, why can't two people both be special and unique? Envy is often the result of fear. Thus, the opposite of envy is *faith* (and gratitude). Faith that:

- There will be enough time, love and attention for you
- There is enough room for others as well as you
- You have enough already (gratitude)
- You *are* enough

So far, we have examined metaphors and models that can improve our self-esteem and self-identity. Spotting unfair comparisons can help us feel better about ourselves – and so can integrity and selfless service to others.

Integrity and service builds self-esteem

According to the psychologist Dr Nathaniel Branden, author of *The Six Pillars of Esteem*, one key pillar of self-esteem is *integrity* – which is the practice of being honest in all your affairs, especially when no one is looking. When you are all alone, you know deep down what you have done. It could be something minor, such as farting and blaming it on the dog. But it could also be something more serious such as theft, fraud or another criminal offence. If you have committed acts of dishonesty, this can later create guilt and shame, which can erode our self-esteem and fuel bad habits (which you'll learn more about in Chapter 3). Thus, one of the ways you can form the opinion of yourself is by acts you have done – even if nobody else knows about them. Conversely, you can build up self-esteem by being honest. So, even if there are negative consequences for telling the truth, at least your conscience will be clearer, and you can give yourself a pat on the back for being truthful. However, it's not a good idea to do this if it would injure others further, or else you risk feeling worse about yourself again.

When faced with the choice between doing the right thing or the selfish and dishonest thing, choosing the former more often will begin to raise your opinion of yourself. Of course, be careful not to fall into the trap of thinking self-care is selfish (it's not). You must put your own oxygen mask on before attempting to assist others; you will not be able to help anyone if you are yourself depleted. Another way to build self-esteem is by doing kind acts of selfless service. In 2011, a study by the psychologist Dr Jennifer Crocker found that selfless acts of service can boost self-esteem.* Thus, an important question to ask yourself is 'Who am I serving?', which will be covered in more depth in Chapters 5 and 6, as being too self-serving can make one more susceptible to depression. An important caveat to note though, as Dr Crocker points out, is that for any service to raise self-esteem, it must be done for the right reasons (i.e. because it's the right thing to do), and not simply just because you're trying to raise your self-esteem or to look good. Serving others is also a way to get more meaning and purpose into your life (an important human need), which we'll cover in the next chapter.

---

* Jennifer Crocker, Amy Canevello and Ashley A. Brown, 'Social Motivation: Costs and Benefits of Selfishness and Otherishness', *Annual Review of Psychology*, 68:1 (2017), 299–325. https://doi.org/10.1146/annurev-psych-010416-044145.

In a nutshell

The key to answering the question of 'How did I form my opinion of myself?' involves firstly looking at how we form our core identity.

Stable v. unstable sources of self-esteem

We may define ourselves by our work, our achievements, or our relationships, but that's clearly shown to be a risky and weak foundation. We have to look beyond our job title and status and look elsewhere to define ourselves – such as character – remembering that this is what real friends like you for. And of course, we must remember that all of us will grow old and wrinkly one day, and that waistlines can expand as well as contract, so it's advisable not to make good looks, physique and fitness level the core foundation of our self-esteem. Some of the most confident people I have met have been the most out of shape physically, and likewise, some of the most insecure people have been in the best shape. Clearly, self-esteem and inner confidence do not have to be contingent on how aesthetically pleasing we are. Of course, there's nothing wrong with wanting to be fit and healthy, and I would highly recommend it! Just make sure it's not the ultimate defining factor of your self-worth.

Less stable sources of self-esteem (External)	More stable sources of self-esteem (Internal)
Job titles	Core identity
Wealth	Identity story
Fame	How we view our imperfections

Less stable sources of self-esteem (External)	More stable sources of self-esteem (Internal)
Romantic partners	How we interpret negative or positive events
Good looks	Our core beliefs
Physique	Our integrity and good deeds
Fitness level	Our conscious awareness of comparison to others

Low self-esteem v. high self-esteem interpretations

We may also form the opinion of ourselves by the events that have happened to us in the past, but it's entirely possible that we are completely wrong in the way we have interpreted those past events with, for example, a pessimistic explanatory style that attributes those events to internal causes (i.e. 'It's my fault' or 'It happened because I was not good enough').

People with low self-esteem	People with high self-esteem
Blame themselves for negative events and outcomes and take too much responsibility.	Look for explanations *beyond* themselves for negative events and outcomes.
Attribute positive events and outcomes to factors outside of themselves, e.g. 'It was just luck' or 'They were just being nice.'	Take credit for positive events and outcomes and see how their contribution or competence made a difference.

People with low self-esteem	People with high self-esteem
'Globalise' negative events; believe a single failure in *one* area of life means they are a failure *on the whole.*	'Localise' negative events; believe a failure in one area of life just affects that *specific* area and does not reflect on them as a whole.

But, as we have seen in this chapter, when you change the interpretation (remembering that 'the map is not the territory'), you change your story and, in turn, change your identity and raise your self-esteem. Re-examine the conclusions you made about past events by asking, 'What other interpretations are there?' It is always worth considering whether you have been subject to the actions or decisions of sick or abusive people (keeping in mind most of society is sick or dysfunctional in some way). In addition, we also saw the importance of noticing how our beliefs may no longer be true today and how they may not even be our own!

We have also seen how trying too hard to be perfect is also a dangerous game to play with your identity and how it's better to actually identify as *imperfect* and to let go of perfection – because it's impossible to avoid making mistakes as a human being! We have also seen how imperfection still has value in superficial material things such as money and property, and likewise in human beings too, and how there is no such thing as failure, only *feedback*.

In addition to our identity and how we explain negative and positive events, what can also play an important part in our psychological well-being is our innate human needs, which we shall explore in the next chapter.

CONTEMPLATIVE QUESTIONS FOR SELF-ESTEEM

Reflect on the following questions:

1. For any events where you have felt that you were bad, shameful or defective, ask yourself:

   i) What other interpretations are there that do not have anything to do with me?
   ii) What may have been going on for the other person?

2. Reflect on the following question:

   'How do I use money, status or achievement to compensate for a lack of self-esteem?'

3. Ask yourself, 'What one good deed will I do for others today?'

CHAPTER 2

Am I Lacking Any Fundamental Needs?

'At the root of every tantrum and power struggle are unmet needs.'

—DR MARSHALL ROSENBERG

There was once a plant who lived in a garden. Over time, it stopped thriving and began to wilt. Now it happened that a person-centred counsellor was walking past, and the plant called out for help. So, the counsellor listened to the plant talk all about its problems, until the sun went down. The plant was pleased that someone would listen, but it was still poorly. The next day, a cognitive behavioural therapist walked past. The plant again cried out for help, so the therapist tried to logically reason with the plant and spot negative thinking patterns in the plant. The plant agreed with some of the logic, but it still didn't get better. The day after, a psychoanalyst happened to be walking past. Again, the plant asked for help, so they began dissecting the plant's childhood, and what it was like to be a seedling. But the plant *still* wasn't thriving – in fact, it started to feel even *worse*, because it didn't have a very loving plant mother or father, and the memories of them were deeply upsetting. The three therapists were stumped at this point, so they called a doctor, who administered strong medication to the plant. It seemed to be doing a little better, but it was still not thriving – and it was starting to have some horrible side effects from the medication. Then, a gardener happened to walk by, saw the poorly plant and noticed that it looked bone dry and was in the shade. So, the gardener helped the plant get some water and relocate into the sunlight. And very quickly after, the plant felt better and began to thrive and blossom again. The plant had spent so long suffering it had totally forgotten its own fundamental needs!

You can provide all the therapy in the world to a plant, but unless it gets its needs met (water and sunlight), and unless it has a healthy environment, it will wilt and die – and the same goes for human beings. This is the basis of human givens psychotherapy: human beings have innate physical and emotional needs, which, if not sufficiently well met, may make them psychologically unwell.* Thus, the reason you may feel unhappy, unfulfilled, low, stressed, anxious or angry, is because your fundamental needs are perhaps not being met. Once you realise this, you then may decide to wisely seek out a therapist or a life coach like me. One of the first things I do with my clients, along with a comprehensive psychometric assessment to determine their character type and core unconscious motivation, is to carry out an Emotional Needs Audit (I have adapted the version developed and used within human givens psychotherapy),† as this rapidly allows me to see what may be making the client so miserable.

The following is my take on the powerful organising ideas

---

* Joe Griffin and Ivan Tyrrell, *Human Givens: The New Approach to Emotional Health and Clear Thinking* (East Sussex: HG Publishing, 2003, 2013).
† https://www.hgi.org.uk/resources/emotional-needs-audit-ena.

that underlie the human givens approach,* some of which I have expressed and expanded in my own way. Broadly speaking, we have biological, social, internal and existential needs, which must be satisfied if we are to be both psychologically and physically healthy.

Biological needs

What separates us from an inanimate object such as a rock is the fact that we have various biological needs that we have to meet in order to stay alive: sleep, nutrition, exercise and physical security. You'd think this would be common sense, but as one coach trainer taught me: *common sense is not necessarily common practice.* Think about how many of us skimp on sleep or exercise because we want to cram in more work or perhaps more partying or socialising. And think about how many of us overindulge in junk food and takeaways, or how long we tolerate unsafe neighbourhoods, homes or partners, or toxic and unsupportive workplaces. Getting the following needs met are essential for mental and physical health.

Some of these may seem like obvious things to be aware of, but it's amazing how many of us don't take care of the basics. I for one didn't start taking these more seriously until I had a mental health crisis of my own!

Quality sleep

As I mentioned in the Introduction, sleep is absolutely vital for peak cognitive and physical condition. World-famous athletes such as basketball player LeBron James and tennis player Roger Federer apparently sleep for an average of twelve hours a night.

---

* https://www.hgi.org.uk/human-givens/introduction/what-are-human-givens.

Meanwhile, record-breaking sprinters like Usain Bolt sleep for around 10 hours.*† *Sleep is for winners*. If you want to win at life, then *sleep*.

While sleep is important for optimum performance, sleep deprivation is *seriously* bad for you. Did you know that even moderate sleep deprivation leads to *cognitive impairment* (diminished ability to think and reason) equivalent to being drunk?‡

Yet, how many of us would show up to work drunk? We may *work* like athletes – pushing ourselves hard, meeting tight deadlines and putting in long hours – but how many of us *sleep* like them? As I have asked various business and start-up owners I have coached, 'What's the most valuable asset in your business?' Ninety-nine per cent of the time they say their clients, their property, their website or their products. 'No', I tell them. 'The most valuable asset in your business is *you* – because if you can't operate, then there is no more business.' And not one client has disagreed with me so far.

Sleep is key for physical and mental health – and for productivity. When we dream, which happens in the phase known as rapid eye movement (REM) sleep, our nervous system gets 'reset'. As psychologist and human givens co-founder Joe Griffin discovered through his research, when we dream, we act out and discharge any 'emotional arousal' accumulated during the day which we didn't express.§ For example, you may have been strongly physically attracted to someone or perhaps jumped at an unexpected loud sound and felt momentarily

---

* https://www.sleep.org/athletes-and-sleep/ – accessed 6 February 2021.

† https://www.espn.com/blog/playbook/tech/post/_/id/797/sleep-tracking-brings-new-info-to-athletes – accessed 6 February 2021.

‡ A. M. Williamson and A. M. Feyer, 'Moderate sleep deprivation produces impairments in cognitive and motor performance equivalent to legally prescribed levels of alcohol intoxication', *Occupational and Environmental Medicine*, 57:10 (2000), 649–655. https://dx.doi.org/10.1136/oem.57.10.649.

§ Joe Griffin and Ivan Tyrrell, *Why We Dream* (East Sussex: HG Publishing, 2006).

fearful. Such events arouse us emotionally and fire up the auto-nomic nervous system for action. But a lot of the time we *don't* take action. We don't say anything to the person we are strongly attracted to, or we realise the loud sound was just a car horn and carry on walking. Still, we need to discharge the arousal that has already taken place, or else we will stay wired for action – and become a bit of a nervous wreck. Discharging emotional arousal happens through dreaming, which is kind of like a software update for the brain and our emotions. Deep sleep on the other hand is when our body heals itself, rebalances neurochemicals, clears debris from our brain and repairs cells. This form of sleep is akin to powering off so that hardware maintenance can be done. After a good night's sleep, we should wake up feeling more energised, motivated and emotionally balanced. However, if we have slept poorly, or in the worst case, not at all, we can be cranky, irritable, lethargic, slow. Not only that, but we can become gluttonous; sleep affects our ghrelin and leptin hormone levels, which are responsible for controlling our appetite. Thus, you may find yourself reaching for more food – especially 'bad carbs' (e.g. highly processed and simple carbohydrates such as white pasta, pizza, crisps, sugary sweets and snacks) – as your body craves the instant energy from the sugar. You're also likely to be more emotional and potentially more anxious, as your nervous system hasn't had a chance to be properly reset.

Thus, one of the best ways you can improve your quality of life, your work performance, your weight management, your physical and mental health is to get better quality sleep, and more of it. One of the biggest mistakes I made as a younger entrepreneur was to think, 'If I sacrifice more sleep, I'll get more done and I'll be more efficient and successful.' The issue of course is that I wasn't operating at my full capacity, akin to making a car run on low fuel. Unfortunately, there's a lot of toxic hustle culture and motivation out there, encouraging people to skimp on sleep in the pursuit of success, to 'grind every day' and take no days off. Management consultants such as Diane Fassel, author of *Working Ourselves to Death: The High Cost of Workaholism*, conclude that this type of masochistic workaholic attitude in organisations in fact costs them *more* in the end due to staff time off from stress, sickness and burnout. So, in the long run, you're not doing yourself or your company any favours.

If you'd like to improve your sleep quality, here are some suggestions on how to do that:

- Avoid caffeine after midday (it has a half-life of six hours, so after twelve hours there's still 25 per cent caffeine content left in your blood).
- Exercise during the day (even going for a walk can be enough).
- Play some relaxing music at bedtime (chillout, ambient and smooth jazz are all good genres for this).
- Avoid overly stimulating video games or TV shows just before bed.
- Keep your room cool, fairly dark and quiet (use earplugs if you have to) – however, if you're childish like me and you don't like the dark, feel free to keep a little bit of warm light in the room!
- Address any worries you have during the day and take proactive action on them (see the Challenging Catastrophising Exercise in the Appendix).
- Do not exercise too close to bedtime.
- Consider using guided relaxation, meditation, hypnosis or prayer to fall asleep.

The bottom line is this: if you want to improve your overall happiness, mood and health, don't skimp on your sleep. And if you find you don't have enough time to sleep, then you are perhaps taking on too much and need to cut back, so that you can. You are otherwise operating at less than your maximum potential and capability, not to mention putting your mental and physical health at serious risk.

Quality nutrition

A well-balanced diet isn't only important for weight management and physical health, *it can also impact mental health.* In the 1990s, a doctor friend of mine said that gut health and diet affects mental health. Her medical colleagues laughed at her. But now she has been vindicated. Researchers and doctors are now suggesting that a healthy diet improves mental health. One study found that a Mediterranean-style diet (a diet high in vegetables, fruits, legumes, nuts, beans, cereals, grains, fish and unsaturated fats such as olive oil) supplemented with fish oil led to a reduction in depression among participants, which was sustained six months after the trial.[*] Another study found that giving multivitamin supplements to trauma survivors of the 2011 earthquake in Christchurch, New Zealand produced significant declines in psychological symptoms and improvements in mood, anxiety and energy (compared to a placebo).[†] Dr David Mischoulon, Professor of Psychiatry at Harvard Medical School, and Director of the Depression Clinical and Research Program of the Massachusetts General Hospital in the US, said that while

---

[*] N. Parletta, D. Zarnowiecki, J. Cho, A. Wilson, S. Bogomolova, A. Villani, C. Itsiopoulos, T. Niyonsenga, S. Blunden, B. Meyer, L. Segal, B. Baune and K. O'Dea, 'A Mediterranean-style dietary intervention supplemented with fish oil improves diet quality and mental health in people with depression: A randomized controlled trial (HELFIMED)', *Nutritional Neuroscience* (2017), 1–14.
[†] Julia Rucklidge, Rebecca Andridge, Brigette Gorman, Neville Blampied, Heather Gordon and Anna Boggis, 'Shaken but unstirred? Effects of micronutrients on stress and trauma after an earthquake: RCT evidence comparing formulas and doses, *Human Psychopharmacology*, 27 (2012), 440–54. https://dx.doi.org/10.1002/hup.2246.

omega-3 fatty acids require more research for efficacy and safety, they are 'promising natural treatments for mood disorders'.*

Many of the foods that feature in the Mediterranean diet could also be good for your mental health because they can boost the amino acid tryptophan, which plays a role in the creation of vitamin B3 (niacin). Vitamin B3 is essential for creating the neurotransmitter serotonin (the hormone responsible for the feeling of well-being, happiness and good mood) as well as melatonin (the hormone responsible for making us feel sleepy at the right time). Foods high in tryptophan include chicken, eggs, cheese, fish, peanuts, pumpkin and sesame seeds, milk, turkey, tofu and soya. Note that in order for tryptophan to be converted into niacin, your body also needs to have enough:

- **Iron** – found in spinach, broccoli, tofu, red kidney beans, edamame beans, chickpeas, nuts, dried fruit, red meat and fish
- **Vitamin B6** – found in peanuts, soya beans, oats, bananas, milk, pork, poultry, such as chicken or turkey
- **Vitamin B2** (also called riboflavin) – found in milk, eggs, mushrooms, plain yoghurt, almonds, avocados, spinach, fortified tofu, beef, salmon

Consuming lots of artificial sugar won't do you much good as it will wreak havoc on your blood sugar levels; low levels can make you moody, irritable and anxious,† while high levels risk making you hyper and edgy. Caffeine can also affect your nerves, as it increases cortisol and adrenaline, and will most likely leave you bouncing off the walls (certainly if you have six cups a day like

---

* David Mischoulon, 'Omega-3 fatty acids for mood disorders', Harvard Medical School – https://www.health.harvard.edu/blog/omega-3-fatty-acids-for-mood-disorders-2018080314414 – accessed 31 March 2021.
† This is most likely where being 'hangry' (hungry-angry) comes from, which is a state of anger caused by hunger.

I used to). One cup of coffee or tea a day may be acceptable, but don't overdo it, and do not drink caffeine after midday, given its half-life of six hours.

And let's not forget alcohol – fine in small doses, alas it can cause hangovers, and when withdrawing from chronic usage, can result in severe anxiety. It slows the nervous system down, meaning you will feel relaxed temporarily, but the effect will wear off and you will go back to your normal state. Alcohol also loosens inhibitions, making it much more likely that you will say or do something you regret – the aftermath of which could leave you with a long-term impact on your mental health, such as a criminal record, drink-driving, or hurting someone you love. I remember I had one client, Sophie, a hard-working city executive, who would get into terrific verbal spats with her partner after a few drinks. There would be much swearing and shouting, and then, the next day, came the guilt, shame and regret (and the hangover). In my own life, I certainly remember getting drunk on occasions, and stuffing myself silly with a takeaway after a night out, and then regretting all those additional calories I packed in, not to mention feeling too lethargic to work out the next day. My mum, who is a police officer, tells me Christmas is a notorious time of year for domestics. With the mixture of dysfunctional families being forced to meet together combined with alcoholic intoxication and loosened inhibitions, it really doesn't surprise me!

Thus, don't expect to be in a great state mentally or physically if you eat lots of junk food and minimal vegetables and have lots of caffeine. And keep in mind a poor diet is linked to all kinds of disease, such as heart disease, hypertension, diabetes, cancer and many more. Health is one of those things we take for granted until we don't have it any more.

And last but not least, let's not forget the importance of staying adequately hydrated. Research shows that being dehydrated by just 2 per cent can impair cognitive function and mental performance (i.e. your ability to problem-solve, memorise, pay attention, and so forth).[*] One study even found that drinking plain water is associated with decreased risk of depression and anxiety.[†]

So what's the long and short of it? Eat your vegetables, get your protein, keep caffeine, refined sugar and alcohol to a minimum, and drink plenty of water. Consider eating low-carbohydrate or at least stick to complex carbohydrates (such as brown bread or brown pasta), as these will give you energy for longer and avoid a carb or sugar crash, and improve your mental and physical health. Of course, seek your doctor's advice on diet before making any changes, especially if you have a medical condition. If you struggle to stick to a sensible diet, then you may have a hidden addiction to food (see next chapter).

Physical exercise

Exercise has a whole host of benefits, not only reducing choles-terol, but also relieving stress, improving sleep and improving mood. In some cases, exercise has been shown to be as effective as antidepressants.[‡§] Thus, if you're feeling low, go for a brisk

---

[*] A. Adan, 'Cognitive performance and dehydration', *Journal of the American College of Nutrition* 31:2 (2012), 71–78. https://doi.org/10.1080/07315724.2012.10720011.

[†] F. Haghighatdoost, A. Feizi, A. Esmaillzadeh, N. Rashidi-Pourfard, A. H. Keshteli, H. Roohafza, and P. Adibi, 'Drinking plain water is associated with decreased risk of depression and anxiety in adults: Results from a large cross-sectional study', *World Journal of Psychiatry*, 8:3 (2018), 88–96. https://doi.org/10.5498/wjp.v8.i3.88.

[‡] Y. Netz, 'Is the Comparison between Exercise and Pharmacologic Treatment of Depression in the Clinical Practice Guideline of the American College of Physicians Evidence-Based?' *Frontiers in Pharmacology*, 8: 257 (2017). https://doi.org/10.3389/fphar.2017.00257.

[§] Harvard Health Publishing (Harvard Medical School), 'Exercise is an all-natural treatment to fight depression', 2013 – https://www.health.harvard.edu/mind-and-mood/exercise-is-an-all-natural-treatment-to-fight-depression – accessed 11 April 2021.

walk, a run or hit the gym. The *worst* thing you can do when you're depressed is to stay in bed all day – as much as you may feel like doing that when you're feeling low in motivational energy. Instead of telling yourself, 'I don't have time to exercise', try reframing this to 'I choose not to prioritise my mental and physical health' and ask yourself, *Is this really true?* Is making money really more important than your sanity? Is meeting everybody else's wants and needs more important than taking care of your own mental and physical health? We never find the time; we must actively create it. Instead of prioritising your schedule, you must schedule your priorities. Read that again. In other words, you may decide that from now on, 7 p.m. to 8 p.m. will be your 'exercise time', or 5 a.m. if you're an early bird. Do some exercise that you actually enjoy. For me, that's usually running and lifting weights. For you, it might be swimming, tennis, yoga or Pilates. Or Quidditch. Whatever floats your boat. Find something that gets you physically active. Remember that you don't have to be an Olympic athlete. Give yourself permission to be bad at it. As long as you enjoy it and it gets you active, that's all that matters. One of my previous coaches was a man in his eighties and he would still go to the gym and play tennis regularly! Of course, sport and fitness is an area of life where many of us could be more self-compassionate, especially as most of us are not training for gold medals or for the military! *Little and often is better than not at all.* If you're struggling with energy levels, perhaps because of burnout or insomnia, just try going for a brief walk outside, even if only for ten minutes.

Time outdoors and in nature

Getting outside serves a number of functions. Firstly, the day-light helps regulate our circadian rhythms. This means it helps us to be more awake during the day, and sleepier at night. Light is important for controlling melatonin and plays a key role in alertness and wakefulness. When we are exposed to light, in particular, bright light, it suppresses melatonin, making us feel more awake and alert, and bright sunlight has been shown to boost serotonin,* which can help us to feel better. Light has even been shown to play a part in beating depression; one study found that exposing depressed people to sunlight was more effective than artificial light, with outdoor light causing a 50 per cent reduction in depressive symptoms.† Note that the brightness (or intensity) of light is measured in lux and is considered to be important in well-being. In one study, it was found that bright light (2,500 lux) had a noticeable antidepressant effect, whereas low intensity light such as from a dim light bulb (300 lux) did not.‡ If you live in the UK (which, let's face it, is not exactly known for its sunny blue skies), you can still get a good dosage of light even if it's overcast outside at around 1,000 lux and thus improve your mental health; you may experience a mild antidepressant effect. Going outside on a sunnier day will expose you to anything from 10,000 lux to 100,000 lux (the latter if you're in direct sunlight). So perhaps a sunny holiday really is what the doctor ordered!

We also get vitamin D from sunlight, and studies have shown that vitamin D deficiency contributes to cancer, heart disease, osteoarthritis, weak bones and rickets. But not only

---

* G. W. Lambert, C. Reid, D. M. Kaye, G. L. Jennings and M. D. Esler, 'Effect of sunlight and season on serotonin turnover in the brain', *Lancet*, 360:9348 7 December 2002),1840–2. https://dx.doi.org/10.1016/s0140-6736(02)11737-5. PMID: 12480364.

† A. Wirz-Justice, P. Graw, K. Kräuchi, A. Sarrafzadeh, J. English, J. Arendt and L. Sand, '"Natural" light treatment of seasonal affective disorder', *Journal of Affective Disorders*, 37:2–3 (12 April 1996), 109–20. https://dx.doi.org/10.1016/0165-0327(95)00081-x. PMID: 8731073.

‡ N. E. Rosenthal, D. A. Sack, C. J. Carpenter, B. L. Parry, W. B. Mendelson and T. A. Wehr, 'Antidepressant effects of light in seasonal affective disorder', *American Journal of Psychiatry*, 142:2 (February 1985), 163–70. https://dx.doi.org/10.1176/ajp.142.2.163. PMID: 3882000.

that – vitamin D deficiency has been linked to depression.*
Furthermore, spending too much time in a small space is not
good for your psyche and can lead to *claustrophobic irritability*,
also known as 'cabin fever'. We were not designed to live in
flats the size of a broom cupboard! But the good news is that
research has shown that even brief interactions with nature
can promote improved cognitive functioning, support a positive mood, and overall well-being. A sunny beach certainly
has a calming effect on me – and many, many English people
alike (which is why many of us flock to countries like Spain for
our holidays). And likewise, some may find the same relaxing
effect with sitting under a tree, walking barefoot on the grass or
hiking in the mountains. Nature is beautiful and can replenish
the mind, body and spirit, especially as many of us begin to
live in increasingly ugly, polluted, industrial and overcrowded
metropolises.

Physical security

Unless we feel physically safe, it's going to be hard for us to
fully relax and let our guard down, and, as such, we will most
likely be anxious and on edge. Our home, local area and place
of work or study need to feel safe. If we do not feel safe, our
amygdala will pump out adrenaline to keep us primed for
fight, flight or freeze. Living in a rough part of town or having
hostile neighbours, flatmates or family members can lead to
hypervigilance and generalised anxiety disorder. If you do
not feel safe where you live, then anxiety isn't a disorder; *it's
a normal reaction to an abnormal situation*, and it may be time
for a move.

---

* R. E. Anglin, Z. Samaan, S. D. Walter and S. D. McDonald, 'Vitamin D
deficiency and depression in adults: systematic review and meta-analysis',
British Journal of Psychiatry, 202 (2013), 100–107. https://doi.org/10.1192/bjp.
bp.111.106666.

Likewise, if you regularly feel unsafe at work because you work in a challenging role such as policing, armed forces, firefighting, psychiatric care, or any job that puts you at risk of physical harm, then it's important that you get enough downtime off duty to allow your nervous system to wind down and recover.

Pay attention to anywhere that makes you feel physically unsafe, whether it's your home, your workplace, your neighbourhood or even your local gym or pub. If this is the case, perhaps it's time to change one, or all, of these, whether that means finding a new job, moving to a quieter neighbourhood out of the city, or even separating from your partner if need be. You're probably reading this book because you want to change your life, right? *If nothing changes, nothing changes.* I didn't feel safe at home, at school or in my neighbourhood growing up, and, as a result, it really did a number on my mental health as a young adult, which required much healing work to remedy.

Social needs

As social beings, we have certain needs that can only be satisfied by other humans. Thus, the idea of total self-sufficiency, I'm afraid, is very much wishful thinking. We need each other; sanity is a group activity. Studies show that those who are isolated and lonely tend to have worse mental *and* physical health.[*] We really do depend on each other to survive! Let's explore what we need from our neighbour:

---

* N. Leigh-Hunt, D. Bagguley, K. Bash, V. Turner, S. Turnbull, N. Valtorta and W. Caan, 'An overview of systematic reviews on the public health consequences of social isolation and loneliness', *Public Health*, 152 (2017), 157–171. https://doi.org/10.1016/j.puhe.2017.07.035 http://www.sciencedirect.com/science/article/pii/S0033350617302731.

Attention

Ever since we were born, we have needed attention. Lack of attention to children is better known as *neglect*, and can result in educational and learning difficulties, low self-esteem, depression, and trouble forming and maintaining relationships and developing social skills. In fact, this need is so important that the lack of attention and affection in babies can not only psychologically distress them, it can also cause their physical growth to be stunted (known as 'failure to thrive'), and in the worst case, attention deprivation can even kill them.[*][†]

Therefore, if any parent says that their child is 'needy', or that 'they're just looking for attention', then they are forgetting that their child is healthy and normal and doing *exactly* what a child ought to be doing. Likewise, as adults, we still need attention; it does not simply vanish. Getting positive attention helps us feel valued, cared for, heard and respected as human beings. Certainly, many of us seem to need this, or else, why would so many share their life on social media? From that point of view, social media may actually be *beneficial* for mental health – provided that the attention received is *positive* (such as affirming and supportive messages and comments). Of course, one must exercise caution not to seek excessive attention (which may be a sign of low self-esteem or other behavioural issues) or become totally reliant on it for one's self-worth.

Friendship

We all need at least one good friend who accepts us as we are, someone to bond with and to, quite literally, help keep us sane.

---

[*] R. Spitz, 'Hospitalism, an inquiry into the genesis of psychiatric conditions in early childhood', *The Psychoanalytic Study of the Child*, 1 (1945), 53–74. doi: 10.1080/00797308.1945.11823126.

[†] H. Bakwin, 'Emotional deprivation in infants', *The Journal of Pediatrics*, 35 (1949), 512–21. doi: 10.1016/S0022-3476(49)80071-0.

What is a good friend? It's someone who unconditionally loves us and who can listen without offering advice, someone who can validate and support us (especially in times of distress, self-doubt or low self-esteem). It's someone who you can be yourself around and someone to share feelings and the ups and downs of life with. Sometimes, as human givens co-founders Joe Griffin and Ivan Tyrrell put it, we need to borrow someone's brain to restore us to sanity, especially when we are hijacked by our own amygdala. Certainly, there have been several times in my life where I have felt low and doubted myself, my worth or my ability. Even yours truly needs a pep talk and some reassurance from a trusted friend occasionally!

The question is, how can we make more friends? Well, there's a whole library of books on that including the classic by Dale Carnegie called *How to Win Friends and Influence People*. However, here are some brief pointers I would give to my clients (and you):

- Friendships are not found – they are *created*
- You will not make more friends unless you take some risks and meet more people
- Start with small talk; no heavy conversation to begin with. Gradually, start to share more about yourself and open up
- Keep an open mind if you are invited to an event (if you're invited to something that you think might be boring or not for you, you never know – you might be pleasantly surprised!)
- Sincere compliments can go a long way
- Look for common interests
- Ask questions and be genuinely interested in others (people love to talk about themselves!)
- Remember others may be just as socially anxious as you are – why do you think so many need a drink at social events?

Intimacy

Intimacy is the *depth* at which we can share about ourselves, our thoughts, our feelings, our memories and what's going in our lives. It is entirely possible to have a lot of friends but to have very little intimacy if you find yourself engaging in a lot of small talk, or you find yourself not being able to disclose very much honestly about your life. This can certainly be the case in big cities at times, because everyone is busy and preoccupied with their own lives, chasing career goals and raising families. Of course, opening up about one's self can feel *risky* – especially if you have been abused, betrayed, mocked or hurt before. Or if you secretly love Comic Sans font, then, sure, perhaps it is better to keep some things to yourself. It can feel safer to stay in a hardened shell, but then you're not living life to the fullest. But not only that – you risk making yourself mentally ill, as intimacy is a fundamental human need. The best thing to do is to gradually and slowly build up intimacy. Some people are safe to be intimate with, others are not. For example, if you find that people reject or mock you as you become more intimate, then it's possible they are not safe to be intimate with or they are simply not compatible with you, and it's better to move on. *You cannot fit a square peg in a round hole.*

Developing intimacy can take time, and for a lot of people, it can be terrifying. But remember: a lake that doesn't occasionally allow fresh water to come in becomes stagnant. *If they don't like you, they're not your tribe.*

Belonging to a wider community

From the dawn of mankind, we have always needed to be part of a tribe. First, as a matter of safety and security; we are much safer when we are looking out for one another and when others can look out for us. Other people also help to stabilise our model of reality and remind us that we are alive. We can create *'layers of belonging'*. For example, I have the following memberships:

- An intimate club for coaches, therapists and psychologists
- Various 12-Step Recovery groups
- A men's self-development and self-defence group
- A WhatsApp group for digital nomads and volleyball players in Tenerife
- An online church

I belong to these groups for various different reasons. These different layers of belonging mean that I have a stronger sense of community, and I get to explore the different facets of my life, such as my professional, spiritual and well-being sides. These different communities bring balance to my life. If I have a rough day, it also means I've got several sources of support. You too can do the same. Perhaps you can join some clubs and communities. The good news is that nowadays, there are communities for pretty much anything, whether it's trainspotting, lacrosse or pug owners. And if you can't find your tribe – *create it*. Start your own club and see who shows up.

Sense of status within social groupings

It's true that we need our own internal self-esteem that is independent of others. But at the same time, just like every other living creature, we can also be affected by our environment and those around us, whether that's in our local area, work or social groups. 'No man is an island', as the author John Donne once wrote. We all need to feel that we have some sort of status. Nobody wants to feel like the runt of the pack, or the clown that isn't ever taken seriously (sadly, both are roles I often felt I fell into in my childhood and early adulthood). This is, of course, unless you happen to have zero ego, in which case, you

are already enlightened and should put down this book immediately to transcend into nirvana. Otherwise, this is another
fundamental need. Note that the wording is 'sense' of status,
which can be affected by how others in the group treat us, the
role we are assigned, and our beliefs and perspectives. Thus,
even if you have a very humble role within a given social group,
it is possible to still have a sense of status with the right mindset,
and if you're treated with respect. Of course, if you are treated
disrespectfully, then your sense of status will be lower. It should
be noted that a sudden drop of status can be quite traumatic and
humiliating (as it was for me!), thus working on a core identity
and true self-esteem beyond status is wise.

Privacy

We all need privacy for several reasons – even if we do not label
ourselves as introverts. Privacy allows us space to consolidate
experiences, think, reflect and process experiences. It allows
us time to 'recharge' from social interactions, and to fully let
our guard down. It also gives us space to have deeply intimate
conversations with those close to us. If you struggle to get privacy where you live, think about where you could have some;
could it be on a walk in the park, in your car, or in the garden
shed? We also need peace and quiet to feel that we have privacy.
Hearing neighbours talking, or unwanted music, especially in
places we deem to be private, can affect our sense of privacy.
If you struggle to get peace and quiet, invest in a good pair of
noise-cancelling headphones; they can make a huge difference!

Psychological needs

As well as getting needs from our external environment and our
community, we also have internal *psychological needs*, which can

be better met and improved by ourselves – even if our external environment is less than ideal.

Self-esteem

We all need to feel that we are inherently worthy as humans. Low self-esteem has a negative effect on various areas of our life, such as work and relationships. If we feel totally worthless, or inherently bad or defective, we can become demotivated, depressed and, in some cases, suicidal. This has sadly been the case of a great proportion of young people. One study carried out by psychiatrists in the US found that 77 per cent of teenagers and children who showed up in A&E with suicidal ideation had experienced bullying, and also that a history of bullying was the most significant predictor of suicidal ideation.[*] Being bullied can certainly lead to low self-esteem because, as explained in Chapter 1, if you have a pessimistic explanatory style, then you are likely to conclude, 'there must be something wrong with me', if someone mistreats you. Low self-esteem also can also lead us to become addicted as we will seek to run away from ourselves (see Chapter 3, 'Am I Running From Anything?').

Sense of autonomy and control

We need to feel that we have some control in our lives, and that we have freedom to make decisions and choices. Even babies need to feel like they have some autonomy, which is why they sometimes choose to turn their head away when you try to feed them. Certainly, in the coronavirus pandemic, many of us had our sense of autonomy and control taken away when various

---

[*] N. Alavi, T. Reshetukha, E. Prost, *et al.*, 'Relationship between Bullying and Suicidal Behaviour in Youth presenting to the Emergency Department', *Journal of the Canadian Academy of Child and Adolescent Psychiatry*, 26:2(2017),70–77. https://www.ncbi.nlm.nih.gov/pmc/articles/PMC5510935/.

lockdowns and restrictions were imposed upon us. This no doubt exacerbated many mental health issues in society, not only because it made it harder to get our innate needs met (such as intimacy and community), but also because it restricted our freedom and control. A useful reframe that one of my coaches once taught me to give me a greater sense of control was the phrase, 'I *choose* to'. For example, rather than thinking, *I have to go to work*, you can think instead, *I choose to go to work, so I can have enough money to pay the bills and live well.* Such a way of thinking allows you to feel more in control and feel less like a helpless victim. Of course, if you don't like your job, then why not empower yourself and take control; get another job or start your own company.

Sense of competence and achievement

We all need to feel that we are competent at life or good at something. Without this, we can feel quite agitated or useless. Of course, if we are hijacked by our amygdala, we may wrongly conclude, *I'm not good at anything!* Is that *really* true? Again, watch out for black-and-white thinking. Perhaps you're good at doing impressions, being creative, listening or being attentive to detail. What have you accomplished in the past? Take an inventory of this. Just be careful, however, not to pin all your worth on how much you have achieved (lest you fall into the trap I did as I shared in Chapter 1).

Fun, play and laughs

One writer, Charlie Hoehn, author of *Play It Away: A Workaholic's Cure for Anxiety*, shared how he had tried just about everything to cure his crippling anxiety: medication, CBT, yoga, meditation, and even psychedelics. Nothing had worked. In the end, after much trial and error, he discovered one thing that did cure his anxiety: *play*.

It's not just Hoehn who needs and benefits from play though. We *all* need to experience some fun and play from time to time, otherwise life will feel like drudgery. It doesn't matter what you do for fun, as long as it's enjoyable and it doesn't harm you or others. Having fun could mean going to the gym and doing exercises you enjoy, playing a video game (in moderation), or doing something creative like singing, painting or writing. Just as long as you do it because you genuinely enjoy it and not because you're simply trying to achieve something. If you feel you have to *force* yourself to do it, then it does not count as fun! Personally, I love to watch TV shows with my best friend Steve together over video chat. I might also play some *Command & Conquer: Generals* (a real-time strategy game). And, in the right mood, I can also find writing genuinely enjoyable too. Make some time, at least once a week, to have some 'you time', to do whatever you find fun and enjoyable.

We can also have fun by having a laugh and cracking jokes. Even in Nazi concentration camps, inmates would joke about each other being skinny. During the coronavirus pandemic, my friends and I would share memes about toilet paper shortages, and so forth. Humour is resilience. My godmother is someone who knows suffering, as she had two children die, grew up in the Second World War, survived a mental breakdown in her youth, and had an extremely abusive mother. And you know what she said in her wise old years? 'You've got to learn to laugh in life.' Laughter really is the best medicine – it releases endorphins and serotonin, which makes us feel happier. Research also shows that people who laugh experience both positive psychological *and* physiological effects.[*] So, if you haven't laughed lately, then why not go and see some comedies? Watch something that will tickle you pink!

------

[*] D. Louie, K. Brook, and E. Frates, 'The Laughter Prescription: A Tool for Lifestyle Medicine', *American Journal of Lifestyle Medicine*, 10:4 (2106), 262–267. https://doi.org/10.1177/1559827614550279.

Sense of financial security

As well as physical security, in this modern society we live in we need to feel that we have financial security too. Why? Because money allows us to buy essentials such as food, clothing and shelter. It can also buy us holidays, meals out, entertainment and, of course, brilliant self-help books like *The 7 Questions*. Money can be so important that some people have committed suicide because of sudden financial hardship, relationships and marriages can become very strained over money troubles, and rifts over financial arrangements can tear families apart (as I know all too well from my own experience).

We need to feel that we have enough money to cover the bills, groceries, housing, as well as a bit of socialising and fun. Otherwise, this can lead to anxiety and stress – as I found out the hard way numerous times over the last ten years as an entrepreneur. During my time at giftgaming, I felt that it was a struggle from day one to stay afloat, and this lasted for several years. First, I had sold all my things and relocated to the Cambridge area with only £3,000 to last me six months. For the first couple of months, I slept on a mattress on the floor in a friend of a friend's house! Eventually, I nearly ran out of money, and didn't have any family money to fall back on. From that point forward the story I had made up (or reinforced) was 'if I work hard enough, I will be safe'. As per the human givens psychotherapy model, when fundamental needs are not met, this can make us mentally unwell. But not only that, unmet needs can make us *addicted.** For example, we can mask a need that is lacking – such as security, belonging or intimacy – through an addiction, such as to alcohol, food or work. The addiction can then cause our other needs to be further neglected, which can make us more

---

* Joe Griffin and Ivan Tyrrell, *Freedom from Addiction: The Secret Behind Successful Addiction Busting* (East Sussex: HG Publishing).

mentally unwell. In my case, my sleep started to get affected as I would work *all night*.

Thankfully, I have learned two very important financial skills: having some money set aside for a rainy day, and monitoring cash flow (what's going out and what's coming in). Both have helped me feel more financially secure. I'm no longer spending down to the wire, which gives me much, much more breathing room. Nothing triggers my workaholism more than the feeling of financial insecurity! In addition, I have learned other tools such as challenging catastrophic thinking, which involves breaking down the steps that lead to the catastrophic outcome.

If you suffer from catastrophic thinking like I do at times, a good question to ask is 'What's my contingency plan if this fear is true?' and 'What happens before the worst-case scenario?' Often, it is not simply a case of running out of money, and then being homeless – at least, not in the UK. You tend to have more options than you think. For example, before you run out of money, you could start cutting back on non-essential expend-iture, such as alcohol, junk food, cigarettes, or meals out. You could then sell some unnecessary possessions, borrow some money from friends, family or even your employer. You could even negotiate your rent (and in the UK your landlord would have to go through a lengthy process before they can evict you, which would buy you more time to find rent money). In the worst case, you could even crash on a friend's sofa for a few weeks like I did!

Now, obviously, I haven't put more money into your bank account. But hopefully what I have done is increase your sense of financial security by showing you that you probably have more of it than you think.

Of course, if you feel your need for financial security is still being threatened, then ask yourself, 'How can I get this need better met?' Perhaps you can make cutbacks on spending, find higher paying work (or increase your rates if you're self-employed), or maybe you could move to a cheaper home or neighbourhood. Perhaps you could also study part-time to get more qualified so that you can command higher rates, or get entrepreneurial and start a side venture. As a last resort, and only after consulting a financial professional, you may also want to consider some sort of low-interest credit facility – but only if you are sure you can make repayments, and if you do not have a compulsive debting problem (repeatedly taking out loans despite extortionate interest rates). Like I said, you often have more options than you think. Only when we are hijacked by our amygdala do we go into the black-and-white thinking of, *I have no options at all! I'm doomed, I tell you, doomed!* When you think like this, you can simply say to yourself humorously, 'Oh, silly amygdala!'

Existential needs

Last but not least, we have an existential need to make sense of life and suffering, as well as hope for the future, or else we'll lose the will and the motivation to live.

Meaning and purpose

Many of us spend much of our life accumulating achievements, wealth and working hard. But to what end? Without meaning and purpose, life becomes nothing more than a disposable, meaningless and very stressful Monopoly game. We get a shiny car, or a hat, maybe a dog, a few houses on Mayfair or Baker Street (if we're extremely lucky), pass go and collect our wages after working fifty or even sixty hours a week, but not before most of it goes on rent, bills, taxes and credit repayments. If we're fortunate, we might also get married (but at least 50 per cent of us will divorce). Eventually, we die at the end of it all; all the pieces go back in the box. Game over.

Is that all there is to life? No wonder we're so depressed. In fact, recent research shows that 20 per cent of people in the UK suffer from anxiety or depression, and depression is also the predominant mental health problem worldwide.* One of the key factors behind depression is *meaninglessness* as shown by various studies – the less meaning one has, the more depression one experiences.† Meaning and purpose are some of the crucial factors that give us motivational energy, and without it, many of us will struggle to get out of bed, but with it, we will be absolutely motivated and driven to achieve incredible things. Later, in Chapter 5, we will explore how you can find more meaningful and enjoyable work, and in Chapter 6, we will cover how you can create more meaning from life in general.

The need for hope in the future

We all need hope for a better future, faith that there is light at the end of the tunnel, or else we can fall into existential despair and despondency – and then depression. For the psychiatrist and Nazi concentration camp survivor Viktor Frankl, the *hope* of seeing his wife again kept him going through the adversity in concentration camps. However, according to Frankl, 'The prisoner who had lost faith in the future – his future – was doomed. With his loss of belief in the future he also lost his spiritual hold; he let himself decline and become subject to mental and physical decay.' Indeed, psychology

---

* J. Evans, I. Macrory, and C. Randall, 'Measuring National Well-being: Life in the UK: 2016', ONS. Retrieved from https://www.ons.gov.uk/people populationandcommunity/wellbeing/articles/measuringnationalwellbeing/ 2016#how-good-is-our-health.
† M. A. Maryam Hedayati and M. A. Mahmoud Khazaei, 'An Investigation of the Relationship between Depression, Meaning in Life and Adult Hope', *Procedia – Social and Behavioral Sciences*, 114 (2014), 598–601. https://doi.org/10.1016/j. sbspro.2013.12.753.

studies show that people with depression often express hopelessness.*

If you have been diagnosed with a chronic illness, if you have suffered a major setback, then you need hope that your future is still bright, and that it will be manageable and that you will still be able to live a good life despite this.

Depressed people are often anxious even if they seem lethargic. There is often huge background anxiety about the future, and usually they have lost hope that their situation or their mental condition will change. According to human givens psychotherapy and Fusion Therapeutic Coaching (a combined approach to coaching and therapy), depression is a *trance state* – just like the one people go into when they are hypnotised. This creates tunnel vision and tricks people into distorted thinking (such as that there is no way out of their hopelessness) because they can't put things into perspective and see the bigger picture. Thus, a highly important element of human givens psychotherapy is to get the client relaxed, so that their emotional arousal goes down and they can see 'beyond the dark tunnel'. The most powerful way human givens therapists and Fusion Therapeutic Coaches do this is through guided imagery (such as guided meditation or hypnosis), which offers the opportunity for the client, while relaxed, to rehearse a different possible future and the steps they need to take to bring it about.

However, calming down by any means can help you get your thoughts back on track. Thus, if you are feeling hopeless, try some deep breathing, guided relaxation, listen to some relaxing music, or call up a trusted friend and share your worries. Next, you may want to have a think about what your options are – we often have more than we think! And remember: *keep it in the day.*

---

* C. J. Nekanda-Trepka, S. Bishop and I. M. Blackburn, 'Hopelessness and depression', *British Journal of Clinical Psychology*, 22: 1, (1983) 49–60. https://doi. org/10.1111/j.2044-8260.1983.tb00578.x.

This means you do not know what the future holds for certain, so live just for *today* and do not worry about tomorrow.

I myself have certainly experienced bouts of hopelessness, which at times has led to depressive (and addictive) episodes. For example, back in 2020 on the night before Christmas Eve in Gran Canaria, I logged on to my online dating profiles to check what exciting dating opportunities awaited me. Unfortunately, as I feared, no replies. No messages. No mutual interest. And more annoyingly, I had no idea *why*. If only I had invented FDBK sooner! Then I would have been able to see perhaps where I might have been going wrong in my dating profile. Was there a photo that was a red flag I wasn't aware of? Was it something in my bio or my photos? Where was I losing women's interest?*

I sighed and longed for some female companionship, and started to despair. Thankfully, I was able to catch myself going into self-blame and I was able to use the re-interpretation exercises described in Chapter 1 to avoid a total self-esteem crash. However, I started to feel *really* sad and hopeless, to the point of where I felt like crying. It had been over three years at this point since I had been in a serious relationship. The voice in my head was very much like a child: *I'll never† get a girlfriend! I'll be alone for ever!* I knew I had to shift my state fast, or soon I would have the urge to start bingeing on food to feel better. First, I remembered the importance of service. So, I began randomly tipping the unsung heroes at the hotel I was staying at; the cooks, the cleaners, the receptionist – the people who probably don't get tipped often. Giving them joy gave *me* joy, and I immediately started to feel better! I then chatted to a few acquaintances (fulfilling my need for connection), and I amusingly watched one of the hotel

---

* These were *exactly* the kind of frustrations that led me to co-found FDBK – see www.fdbk-app.com/about to learn more about why I started it.
† 'Never' and 'always' are often give away signs that we are being hijacked by our amygdala (which thinks in black-and-white ways under stress).

staff members attempt to set up a toy train in a Christmas display as it zoomed around in a circle and kept crashing (getting my need for fun met!). After I had calmed down, I snapped out of the mild depressive trance I was in. I remembered to 'keep it in the day'. I had gone into doom-and-gloom catastrophic thinking and fortune-telling into the future, all on the back of not receiving any dating interest that day. Silly amygdala!

In a nutshell

If you have all your innate needs adequately met, you will be well on your way to not only being mentally and physically healthy, but also living a wholesome, enjoyable and fulfilling life. A question you need to continually ask yourself is not only, 'Am I lacking any fundamental needs?', but also, 'How can I get these needs met?', as we cannot get all of our needs met by just thinking about them; we also need to take some proactive action too. Sometimes we need to act our way into right thinking, rather than trying to think our way into right action: we need to take proactive and practical steps to change our psychological state, rather than just trying to think differently. If you struggle with taking action or socialising (because of social phobia or anxiety), then this is where working with a coach or a therapist might be really helpful.

If you're feeling low, empty, or just feel like something is missing, perhaps you need to ask yourself if you're lacking exercise, friendship, a good laugh, a bit of fun, or a connection to a purpose greater than yourself. There may also be a lack of meaning in your life, or no hope for the future (this can also be because of your beliefs, which Chapter 7 will explore further). Keep in mind that without meaning, purpose and hope, we can very quickly lose motivational energy and think, *Why bother?*, which can lead to depression!

In the next chapter, we will explore how unmet needs as well as various other factors can cause us to start using bad habits to cope.

GROWTH ACTION

Get your fundamental human needs met

Grade the following innate human needs out of 10 (with 10 being that the need is totally met):

- **Quality sleep** – how refreshed and recharged do you feel in the morning, do you rely on natural energy or caffeine and sugar?
- **Nutrition** – healthy, balanced diet – minimal processed sugars, alcohol and caffeine
- **Physical exercise** – exercising at least 3 times a week
- **Time outdoors** – getting enough sunshine and fresh air
- **Self-esteem** – how worthy and lovable do you feel?
- **Physical security** – safe home, neighbourhood, work, etc.
- **Financial security** – enough to pay the bills, live well, socialise
- **Attention** – from colleagues, friends, family, peers – a form of emotional nutrition
- **Sense of autonomy and control** – feeling in control of your life and choices
- **Belonging to a wider community**
- **Friendship and intimacy** – to know that at least one other person accepts us totally for who we are

- **Privacy** – opportunity to reflect and consolidate experience
- **Sense of status within social groupings**
- **Sense of competence and achievement**
- **Fun and play** – having fun and laughs, time for recreation and enjoyment
- **Meaning and purpose** – clear life purpose or mission, doing meaningful work, being challenged
- **Hope for the future** – hope that things will get better, that your situation isn't permanent, that good things are to come

Now ask yourself:

1. What could I do to improve my lowest scores?
2. What tiny steps will I take to get these needs met?

CHAPTER 3

Am I Running From Anything?

'The dark thought, the shame, the malice,
meet them at the door laughing,
and invite them in.'

—RUMI

There was once a man who ran across a busy road. It gave him such an adrenaline rush! He loved it so much, he continued to run across the busy road for several more years. But over time, he started to get clipped by a few cars, and got some scrapes and bruises as a result. Still, he found himself wanting to go back out into the busy road. 'I can handle this, I just need to be more careful,' he told himself. He continued running across the busy road and getting bruises, until one day, a car finally knocked him over. Luckily, it hadn't been going that fast, and he escaped with just a broken arm. But still, he didn't want to give up this behaviour despite having his arm in a sling – it felt so good! Again, he told himself, 'I'll be more careful,' and off he went across the busy road. Despite trying to be more careful, he got hit again, only this time, he wasn't so lucky; a car ploughed into him at great speed and hit him with such force that he was sent flying in the air. As a result, he ended up with several broken bones and was paralysed from the waist down and now he needed to use a wheelchair. He could no longer work, and his partner was tired of his antics and so they left him. And yet, he *still* believed that if he could just manage things more carefully, he could continue his practice of running across busy roads. Despite pleas from his friends and family to stop, he would not. He decided to take his wheelchair across the busy road for just one more thrill . . . Sadly, he could not wheel fast enough to avoid the six-tonne truck that came out of nowhere. And that was the end of that man.

If you have a 'bad habit', you may in fact be *addicted*. 'Addiction' can seem like a dirty and dramatic word, one that is perhaps reserved for the homeless crack addict, or the park bench drunkard. But simply put, *an addiction is repeating a behaviour because it provides relief, despite negative consequences.* How many of us have overindulged in food despite gaining weight and feeling guilty or ashamed by our expanding waistlines and countless failures to stick to a healthy balanced diet? How many of us have worked a bit too hard and too much to the detriment of our health or our relationships? And how many times have we said 'never again' only to find ourselves repeating the same pattern? The truth is, all of us are on some kind of addictive spectrum. How can we not be? Anything that gives us pleasure, be it food, sex, love, video games, social media, coffee, exercise or work, has the potential to become a crippling addiction as it can provide relief or a high, and can easily become a form of escapism from reality.

Most addictions are not caught until it's too late – not until there's a major crisis, such as a health diagnosis, a mental break-down, an ultimatum from a partner, a divorce, being fired from a job, a criminal conviction, or an admission to rehab. At this point, much damage has been done – some of which may be irreversible. Unfortunately, our ego and pride often get in the way of admitting we have a problem. And, of course, so does the high from the addiction too, because pre-recovery, it seems like it has more pros than cons – so why quit? However, ignoring a problem habit is like ignoring the warning light on a car dashboard ... it's fine until one day, the car decides to go haywire and the brakes don't work at a time when you most need them to, which could have been avoided had you taken the time to address the problem earlier.

Admitting you have a problem

In addition to my workaholism, I struggled with overeating and bingeing on junk food. As a result, my weight and physique has yo-yoed over the years. I tried numerous things, yet my willpower always failed me. What really started to shift things (and shift some weight!) was when I finally admitted that I was addicted to food. It might sound like I'm being dramatic, but I'm not. When we eat, our brain rewards us with a hit of dopamine for getting our fundamental needs met and that, in turn, makes us feel good. But when we start bingeing or using food to run from emotions such as loneliness, anger, or sadness, we are misusing food. Food and work addiction can be harder to spot, because unlike drink and drugs, we need food to survive, and most of us cannot live without working. They are less obvious – and more so with food addiction, a problem which I believe is severely underdiagnosed especially in the UK. The only sign of a problem *externally* might be weight gain, and the Health Survey for England 2019 estimates that nearly two-thirds of adults in England are overweight (36.2 per cent) or obese (28 per cent)!* This is incredibly alarming, as

---

* House of Commons Library, UK Parliament, 'Obesity Statistics', 2021: https://commonslibrary.parliament.uk/research-briefings/sn03336/ – accessed 24 March 2021.

being obese or overweight increases the risk of diabetes, high blood pressure, strokes, heart attacks and heart disease,[*] as well as decreasing immunity to general disease.[†]

Anything that gives us some kind of pleasure can become addictive and make our lives unmanageable. But it would take several more attempts of me saying 'I can control this' and 'I just have to manage this better' before I finally accepted that I had a problem. Often it is not until someone hits rock bottom that they become ready to surrender and truly change. Paradoxically, by admitting I am powerless over my addictions, I gain more power and more control over my life. Every day, I have to stay vigilant and avoid the foods that can trigger me into a 'bingeing episode'. If I have my trigger foods, they will most likely send me on a bender, much like someone with alcoholism who has one drink and then goes on a drinking spree. I do not try to think, *I can surely manage just a little bit of cake!* That would be akin to someone with a cocaine addiction saying, 'I can manage a smidge of coke!' or someone with alcoholism saying, 'I can manage a few sips of beer!' In the next Growth Action exercise, you'll find a series of questions to determine if you too might have an addiction.

GROWTH ACTION

Determine if you have a hidden addiction

Think of a 'bad habit' or negative behaviour you have and answer the below honestly:

---

[*] British Heart Foundation, 'Obesity', https://www.bhf.org.uk/informationsupport/risk-factors/your-weight-and-heart-disease – accessed 29 March 2021.
[†] C. J. Andersen, K. E. Murphy and L. M. Fernandez, (2016) 'Impact of Obesity and Metabolic Syndrome on Immunity', *Advances in Nutrition* 7:1 (2016), 66–75. https://doi.org/10.3945/an.115.010207.

1. Does this behaviour provide a feeling of temporary relief, comfort or some sort of high?
2. Are there negative consequences after doing this behaviour?
3. Have you been unable to stop this behaviour despite your best efforts?
4. Has your behaviour ever been pointed out by loved ones, friends, family or professionals?
5. Do you feel at all defensive or angry when you are asked to stop or cut down on the behaviour in question?
6. Do you feel you need to do the behaviour in order to feel better or 'feel alive'?
7. Do you often think about doing this behaviour even when you are not doing it?
8. Do you consider the behaviour 'a bad habit'?
9. Have you been concerned at all about the behaviour in question?
10. Have you ever felt out of control or that you 'crossed the line' at all doing the behaviour?
11. Do you find yourself 'bingeing' or alternating between overindulgence and avoidance with the behaviour?
12. Do you find yourself thinking, *I just need to moderate my usage* about this behaviour?
13. Have you ever needed to lie or cover up for doing the behaviour?
14. Do you find yourself needing to do the behaviour more and more often, or at increasing levels of intensity to get the same sense of relief or pleasure?
15. Do you say to yourself *I will stop tomorrow* or *This is the last time* only to find that you never do?

16. Does life without this behaviour or choice of substance feel unimaginable, impossible, unbearable or even frightening?

17. Do you find yourself increasingly neglecting sleep, nutrition, finances, self-care or loved ones in order to carry out this behaviour?

18. Do you find that once you start the behaviour or using the substance, it's very hard to stop?

19. Do you feel a 'magnetic pull' to this behaviour or substance – especially when feeling strong emotions such as fear, anger, loneliness or stress?

20. Do you feel you can never 'have enough' of this behaviour or substance?

If you have answered 'yes' to three or more questions, it is likely that this 'bad habit' is an addiction.

Assessing the damage

After completing the previous Growth Action, you may have identified that this 'bad habit' of yours is actually an addiction. Now, it's time to reflect on the following:

- How much has this addiction cost you:
  - Weekly?
  - Monthly?
  - Yearly?
  - Over the last 5/10/20 years?
  - What could you have done with the money instead?

- How has this addiction affected:
  - Your health?

- Your psychological well-being?
- Your career and work?
- Your family?
- Your relationships?
- Your overall happiness?

Are you willing to go to any lengths to quit?

In order to beat this addiction, you have to be willing to go to *any* lengths to do so. That may mean avoiding certain triggering scenarios or activities or doing things you wouldn't have dreamed of doing before. Are you ready to make this commitment?

* * * *

*Are you willing to go to **any** lengths to be free of your bad habit?*

Make a decision now, then continue reading.

* * * *

Taking radical action

So, are you willing to go to *any* lengths? If so, congratulations –
you have made an important and life-changing decision – and it's
now time for some *radical action*. Radical action means making
some extraordinary and maybe even some extreme changes –
even if people think you're crazy. Remember: *if nothing changes,
nothing changes.*

For example, despite the fact that I have been doing computer
programming since I was thirteen years old, and have a first-class
degree in Computer Science, I have decided to no longer do it.
Not only that, but I'm *still* paying back my student loan at the
time of writing this for the privilege of studying for said degree!
But this is my way of taking radical action and I have found it's
completely necessary if I want to stay sober from work addiction.
Programming triggers my workaholism and perfectionism to the
point where I won't eat, sleep or even take bathroom breaks
until my code is working! This is seriously unhealthy. For me,
programming is like crack cocaine. Thus, I let my technical co-
founder take care of anything relating to app coding for FDBK.

I also no longer buy things like peanut butter (despite the
fact it was one of my favourite foods), because I know I'm likely
to eat it straight from the jar if I'm under stress and therefore
pack in too many calories. In fact, I keep very little food in my
apartment except for low-fat protein yoghurt and cottage cheese,
because there's very low risk of me bingeing on such foods. I also
do not generally buy or eat things like sweets, chocolate bars,
cakes, ice cream or pastries as these are all trigger foods for my
food addiction. I must avoid these foods to stay a healthy weight
and avoid food binges. I am also completely teetotal because I
know that alcohol loosens my inhibitions and will make me go
on a bender with junk food (and even indulge in smoking!). Such
are the sacrifices I must make to stay on the path of recovery,
sanity and wellness. How about you – are there people, places,

activities or things that trip you up back into your bad habits? If so, it's time to cut them out, or at least, just for today.

Another important part of taking radical action is to start taking inventories of what you're running away from, which we will cover next.

GROWTH ACTION

Take radical action

1. Reflect on the following:

    i) Which people, places, activities or things do you find trigger you back into your bad habit?
    ii) How radical would it be if you were to stop seeing those people or doing those activities?

2. Now go ahead and take radical action.

What we run away from

My guidance will help you to see if you are using a bad habit to run away from something within you. For example, you might drink, eat, work or play video games too much. Perhaps you have a problem with returning to toxic people or relationships. Maybe you have a secret overeating, overspending or debting problem. Whatever the habit is, it's most likely a symptom: *there's something you are running from.* So, in order to help reduce or cut out any bad habit, we must bring to conscious awareness exactly what we are running from – and why.

As you will discover, the main things that we run away from are:

- Unmet fundamental needs (see Chapter 2)
- Stress
- Trauma
- Low self-esteem
- Resentment
- Fear
- Guilt

After reading this chapter, you'll be able to take an inventory of these things and address them head-on so that they do not unconsciously drive your behaviours any more. You will discover why, at times, your bad habits seem very tempting – no matter how much willpower you have.

Running from unmet needs

As explained in the previous chapter, getting our fundamental needs met is essential for mental and physical health. However, when our needs go unmet, we can start to turn to unhealthy behaviours and substances in order to compensate. Thus, all addiction ends in clinical depression because, piece by piece, it prevents your innate human needs from being met, and you become like a wilted plant, starving for water and sunlight.

Addiction is a form of temporary insanity; when we are deep in its throes, only the fix – the high – matters. And nothing else. In some ways, it's almost like a hypnotic *trance*. Have you ever stayed up late bingeing on a TV series, a video game, or perhaps a really engaging book? You were probably in a hypnotic trance then. For a while, being in that trance-like state or that 'reality distortion bubble', might offer a temporary reprieve from the pressures and stressors of life. Perhaps it's overindulgence in junk food, a late-night TV series marathon, a bottle of wine, or an impulsive decision. For a while it might feel good. But then the bubble bursts and reality hits home, and then there are consequences, such as weight gain, health issues, financial loss, hurt people and hangovers. These consequences take us further away from being able to meet our needs, and so now the addictive bubble becomes even more alluring. *Lonely?* Have another pint of ice cream. *Feel life is meaningless?* Have another beer. *No hope that things will get better?* Watch another episode. This vicious cycle is what makes addiction so hard to break using only one's own willpower.

Certainly, in my case, I had to undergo a lot of learning, mentoring and coaching from others before I could really start to get a handle on my own bad habits and addictions – and even then, recovery isn't a destination, but an ongoing journey. I know I must keep my humility because otherwise I risk having a major relapse; I might burn out and break down again, or gain another 25 kg as I did by the end of 2019 because I was so busy working and not meeting my biological need for quality nutrition and adequate sleep. Even the most efficient machines will break down if you do not give them enough care and maintenance. As I tell some of my high-performance clients: they need to become like F1 cars, which need tyres changed and refuelling regularly, or else they don't operate at their highest performance level. Furthermore, they still need to cool off once in a while, and have their oil changed, as well as have occasional repairs too. Now, if *non-living* machines need this, how much more do us living and social human beings need? To operate like an F1 car as a human means plenty of rest, naps, time off, fun and laughs, connection, attention, belonging and privacy. These are not luxuries; they are absolute necessities if we want to stay mentally healthy and fit, and if we want to stay abstinent from bad habits. As well as avoiding having unmet needs, we also want to avoid states of prolonged and severe *stress*.

Running from stress

Dr Patrick Carnes, a world-renowned expert on addiction, says that addiction and high stress are 'inextricably connected', and refers to the process of addiction as a 'maladaptive response to stress'. In other words, people turn to their addictions as an attempt to self-medicate stress. Stress can accumulate as the result of a number of things, such as unmet needs, resentments and sick environments (which we will explore later). Sometimes, though, it is much, much simpler.

Overscheduling leads to stress (and addiction)

Do you find yourself rushing around, with barely any time to breathe or think? Nothing gets our hearts racing and adrenaline pumping like running late. The car or person in front of you suddenly seems to be going a bit too slow. *Why won't they just bloody go faster?* Before you know it, you're raging to yourself, and you're feeling stressed out. You frantically scramble and only make it in the nick of time. Perhaps you arrive to the meeting late, but there's no time to dwell; you have *another* meeting booked back to back. While on your way to that meeting, you receive three emails with 'urgent' tasks that you need to do, and then a phone call from your boss (or your client) with another 'urgent request'. By the end of the day, you are so frazzled, that the addictive behaviour to 'just take the edge off' seems all the more alluring. 'I've earned this after the day I've had!' you might say to yourself. Certainly, this has been my own experience. For example, when I was a young entrepreneur, I would be rushing through a busy day of travelling and meetings, and then I would unwind with unhealthy treats.

Nowadays though, I typically allow an hour between client sessions, so I have time to decompress, relax and refuel. Of course, if you do not have this luxury, then see what boundaries you can put in place with your work. *If you do not set your boundaries, others will control and take advantage of you.* Setting boundaries might look like:

- Turning off your phone when you get home or travel
- Saying no to requests for overtime, favours or other commitments or projects if you're already stretched
- Not checking work emails in the evening

Of course, some of us work in roles which are, by their nature, more stressful and adrenalising than others, such as working in emergency services and the armed forces. If this is the case, make sure you're getting adequate downtime between shifts or being on call. Where possible, allow more time for tasks and travel, and avoid back-to-back meetings. Ask yourself, 'Am I trying to achieve too much in one day?' Be careful not to buy into that toxic 'hustle and grind' and 'no days off' culture. Remember: *being busy and being productive are not the same thing.*

One thing to keep in mind is that stress can also be caused not only by modern twenty-first-century living, but also by *trauma*.

Running from trauma

One thing you may be running from is *trauma*. Trauma is not limited to just soldiers of war, or victims of sexual assault, or car crash survivors (big traumatic events like these are referred to as 'Big T' trauma by psychotherapists). Trauma can be anything that threatens our fundamental human needs such as:

- The loss of financial security
- The loss of a friendship or relationship
- Bullying (physical and emotional security threatened)

Such events are referred to as 'little t' trauma by psychotherapists. On their own, they may not be so traumatic, but repeated or prolonged 'little t' trauma can affect our mental health via post-traumatic stress.

If you suspect you may be running from trauma, it is worth working with a suitably qualified professional trained in one or more techniques, including:

- *The Rewind Technique* – involves rewatching the trauma in your imagination while in a relaxed state and rehearsing a new response to potentially triggering future scenarios in your imagination.
- *EMDR (Eye Movement Desensitisation and Reprocessing)* – involves following a light back and forth horizontally with your eyes while recalling a trauma. This causes your eyes to move in such a way that you stimulate both the left (logical) and right (creative and feeling) brain hemispheres, such that the left can 'speak to' the right. The other reason why EMDR works is because following the lights somewhat while recalling the traumatic memories acts as a form of exposure therapy.
- *Bioenergetics and Trauma Release Exercise* – which is like psychotherapy for the body. The 'Bow' exercise in bioenergetics is particularly useful in causing your body to involuntarily shake. To do the Bow, you use your hands to push your lower back forward. Then you stretch your arms up – and become like a bow. As you do so, continue breathing, and you may notice your core starting to shake. The idea is that this involuntary shaking is what animals do in the wild after being attacked, and it helps reset their nervous system by burning off excess cortisol and adrenaline.
- *Post-induction Therapy* (PIT) – the practitioner puts you in a hypnotic state and has you revisit the traumatic

memory, usually as a 'functional adult' who is grown up, and you have an imaginary conversation with your younger self, so that you develop a new relationship with the traumatic memory.

Note that a pure cognitive-behavioural (intellectual) approach is unlikely to be effective because of how trauma works; the amygdala holds the traumatic memory and constantly scans the environment for anything that even remotely resembles the memory (known as 'pattern matching'). If there is a pattern match, the amygdala sounds the alarm (which in phobias and PTSD, is a false alarm), much like a sensitive smoke detector going off to burnt toast. Thus, merely talking about trauma can in fact re-traumatise you if you (or your therapist) generates the pattern match, and most likely it won't do much to take the emotional charge out of the memory or shift the memory from the amygdala into the 'long-term storage' area of the brain.

Trauma can be difficult to heal because, firstly, no psychological technique is ever 100 per cent effective, and, in addition, the effectiveness of any trauma reduction technique will depend on how strong your relationship is with your practitioner (as well as how well they carry it out). However, on the long road to healing from trauma, practising the following may help:

1. Regular guided relaxation – such as with self-hypnosis, guided meditation or even guided prayer – this will help bring down your emotional arousal level and anxiety.
2. Regularly connecting with others who are gentle and loving and leave you feeling accepted and loved (and avoiding people, situations or places that trigger you too much).
3. Avoiding caffeine (as this will put you more on edge as it increases cortisol and adrenaline levels).

4. Avoiding alcohol (it often can leave you feeling more anxious and nervous after you come down from the high).

5. Staying connected to a purpose greater than yourself and focus on serving others.

6. Avoiding victim mentality (instead of asking 'why me?', asking 'what now?').

7. Regularly and consciously slowing down and deepening your breathing to activate the relaxation response in your nervous system. Try breathing in for four seconds and breathing out for eight seconds using only your belly (this is known as 'diaphragmatic breathing'). If you lie down and put your phone or a pebble on your belly button, as you breathe in and out, see if you can get it to go up and down.

8. Listening to relaxing music (one study found that it can improve the sleep of traumatised people).*

9. Living in smaller and quieter places with fewer people, which are less stimulating and taxing for the nervous system than busy, loud and aggressive cities.

10. Using earplugs or active noise-cancelling (ANC) headphones if you struggle to get peace and quiet. People with trauma and post-traumatic stress can be very sensitive to, or easily irritated by, unwanted noise, which can create stress, giving more ammunition to addiction.

In addition to trauma, you might be also running from low self-esteem.

---

* K. V. Jespersen and P. Vuust, 'The Effect of Relaxation Music Listening on Sleep Quality in Traumatized Refugees: A Pilot Study', *Journal of Music Therapy*, 49:2 (Summer 2012), 205–29. doi: 10.1093/jmt/49.2.205. PMID: 26753218.

Running from low self-esteem

We can also be running from low self-esteem and feelings of worthlessness and unlovability. This is a painful place to be; who wants to experience the feeling of being totally worthless, useless and unlovable? Of course, if you are thinking that you have absolutely *zero* worth and there's *nothing* lovable about you, then, most likely, you are being hijacked by your amygdala, because you are thinking in black-and-white terms with all-or-nothing thinking. Really? There's absolutely *nothing* redeemable about you at all? If this is the case, you first need to calm yourself down, whether it's through deep and slow breathing, or speaking to someone you trust. In a word, your amygdala is running the show – not your rational, thinking brain! You are also most likely being enslaved by the story you created from the past.

You may be unnecessarily blaming yourself for rejections or things not going your way – much like I did. For example, when I found that I wasn't getting mutual interest from people I liked on dating sites. It's worth remembering, of course, that people may use online dating and dating apps for other purposes such as:

- Window-shopping (browsing without real intent)
- To gain a validation boost and see how many likes they can get
- To gain followers on social media (some users ask you to message them on certain platforms which suspiciously requires you to follow them first in order to do so)

In online dating, a person may also not reply for a number of reasons that do not involve you:

- They may secretly be in a relationship already
- They may not be a fully paid member and the dating platform may not permit them to respond
- They may not find you attractive without there being anything wrong with you*

Remember what I said in Chapter 1; *one of the best ways to improve your self-esteem is to stop blaming yourself.*

If you are still battling with low self-esteem, go back to Chapter 1 and complete the Growth Actions. Challenge the stories you have created from the past and look for other interpretations that don't involve you. Note that low self-esteem can also be created by beliefs from intense emotional experiences which may require the help of a good life coach or a therapist to help you shift.

Next, we shall look at resentments, fear and guilt, which can also feed addictions.

Running from resentments

In Alcoholics Anonymous's *The Big Book* (the main textbook of AA which underpins most other 12-Step programmes), there is an important line: 'Resentment is the number one offender [for relapse]. It destroys more alcoholics than anything else.'

Certainly, this has been true in my life; whenever I have felt angry, I noticed I felt very stressed, and I started to seek to relieve that stress, often in not very helpful or healthy ways before I entered recovery, such as by overeating, overworking, overindulging in video games and, occasionally, a whole bottle of wine. This is because resentment causes anger, and anger is

---

* Case in point: I'm rarely attracted to blonde women for some reason, whereas I seem to have a particular weakness and fondness for brunettes.

a state of intense emotional arousal, which when experienced, causes the amygdala to run riot over our more rational thought processes. But in a lot of cases, an amygdala hijack – or an 'anger attack' – can be very damaging to our health and put us at risk of a heart attack, high blood pressure, or our actions arising from that anger could result in a criminal record, a prison sentence, permanently damaged relationships, or a relapse in addictions or bad habits. If you have an addictive behaviour, whether it's overeating, drinking or working too much, you will definitely want to avoid making decisions or being in stressful situations when you are *HALT*: Hungry, Angry, Lonely or Tired. Such states will cause us to be more emotionally aroused and more irrational, making a slip, a relapse, or a regrettable action or comment, more likely.

Calming our amygdala down first

In intense emotional states, we do not behave or think rationally, so we first need to calm down, although I do not recommend telling an angry person (except from yourself) to do so! In his book *The Chimp Paradox*, the psychiatrist Steve Peters explains that we have an 'inner chimp' (which some psychotherapists call an 'inner child') that hijacks us when we feel strong emotions. When a chimp is angry, you don't try to contain it in a cage straight away otherwise it will pummel you to death with its greater strength. Instead, you *exercise* it and tire it out first. Similarly, you don't attempt to have a rational conversation with a young child who is screaming and crying! You first need to calm the child down, which is often done with physical and emotional reassurance, and soft tones. Here are some ways to calm your inner child/chimp down:

1. *Physical exercise*: when we are primed for 'fight' response (often when we are angry), this can ready

us for physical action. Thus, going for a run or lifting some weights can be a good way to discharge the adrenaline. However, be careful using a punching bag when angry. The psychologist Joe Griffin believes this will lead you to conditioning yourself to punch every time you're angry – which may not be ideal!

2. *Clenching your fists*: clench them hard until they are white while breathing in. Then, breathe out slowly and release them to the count of ten. You can also progressively tense up other muscles in your whole body and do this exercise. Slowing down your breathing and making the outbreath longer than the inbreath is also a good way to activate the relaxation response in your nervous system.

3. *Venting to a friend*: sometimes we just need to be heard and acknowledged in our pain. Call up someone to express how angry you feel and to vent your frustration. This is where having a support group like a 12-Step Recovery programme, a coach or therapist, or even a good friend can help. Just make sure that the person you call can empathetically listen without offering unsolicited advice, as otherwise this could make you *even angrier.**

Taking a 'Moral Inventory'

Once we are in a calmer state of mind, we can then start to reframe things so that we are less angry. Professor Peters would call this 'boxing the chimp', while some psychotherapists might

---

* Case in point: I used to have some terrific arguments with an ex-girlfriend because whenever I called her for support, she would launch into 'coaching mode' and try to make me see 'the other viewpoint', rather than give me space and support. I would then complain, 'You *never* give me empathy!' Notice the all-or-nothing thinking, showing I had been amygdala-hijacked.

call this 're-parenting the inner child'. We can do this by taking a *Moral Inventory*, which is a fantastic tool I learned from 12-Step Recovery that helps to reduce the impact of powerful and toxic emotions such as resentment. Resentments can stay embedded in our unconscious mind for a long time and can keep us bitter and twisted. One day if you are reminded of the resentment, or another event happens similar to the resentment-inducing situation, this could trigger stress and anger (because of the fast pattern-matching amygdala), which could then make that bad habit seem all the more alluring. To do a Moral Inventory, you start by drawing up four columns:

1. **Who I resent**
2. **Why**
3. **Which parts of self were affected**
4. **Resentment reduction**

In Column 1 (*Who I resent*), you write who you resent. Easy. This could be a person, or an organisation.

In Column 2 (*Why*), you write down why you resent them. For example, you might resent someone because they might be more physically in shape than you, or they were inconsiderate to you.

In Column 3 (*Which parts of self were affected*), you write down how your resentment affected you. It may have affected your pride, ego, self-esteem, serenity, emotional security, personal relations, finances, ambitions – or all of these.

One sunny afternoon during the Covid-19 lockdown, as I was trying to work from home, I kept hearing, *thump, thump, thump.* Yet again, the neighbour across the road was blasting out his music. So, I went over for the umpteenth time and asked if he could turn the music down. I also explained that if I kept hearing it, I would report it to the council. This made him irate, and he began threatening me and swearing at me. When I got back into my house, I was furious. Once I had calmed down, I then commenced to do a Moral Inventory and wrote down the following:

1. **Person:** *Neighbour across the road*
2. **Why:** *Plays his music too loud constantly! Was very unreasonable, threatening*
3. **Which part of self was affected:** *Pride, ego, self-esteem, serenity, emotional security, personal relations, finances, ambitions*

My pride, ego and emotional security were bruised from how my neighbour spoke to me. The music disturbed my serenity, which I was irritated about, and when I'm agitated, I'm also not great with people, so it affected my personal relations. It also affected my work, which, in turn, affects my finances and ambitions. Lastly, my self-esteem took a bit of a hit; I felt a bit of a coward that I was not 'tough enough' to confront him again. However, as per my psychoeducation training on anger, walking away was probably the smart move in this case!

Finally, in Column 4 (*Resentment reduction*), you do some reflecting and writing to quell the anger. You can do this using one of the following *Resentment Reduction Questions*. These questions will help you rethink and re-examine your feelings and help take some, if not all, of the charge out of the resentment.

Resentment Reduction Question #1:
What was my part in this?

In Chapter 1, we focused on the importance of not blaming yourself when someone's behaviour is abusive or toxic. And indeed, that still applies. However, in order to avoid being a totally helpless victim, and to recognise any negative patterns in your own behaviour, it can also be empowering to see where you may have co-created the resentment by asking yourself, 'What was my part in this?'

Certainly, with some previous coaches and mentors I worked with, some of them were abusive at times, and I could have avoided developing resentments towards them had I not picked them in the first place. I realise now though that my part was that I would pick coaches and mentors based on how superficially impressive their 'coaching CV' was – I would go for people who *looked* good on paper rather than people I got along well with. Therefore, I take some responsibility in that and I own it. And, as such, my resentment towards them has reduced.

But what about the noisy neighbour across the road? Perhaps my part might have been that I have unrealistic expectations about London being a quiet city. Thus, my expectations were part of the problem. I also realised that another thing I did was I took the music being played as if it were directed against me *personally*, rather than seeing it as a nuisance towards the entire neighbourhood. So, I was perhaps quite self-centred in that regard.

You may not have a part to play in creating the event that led to a resentment arising (such as with certain traumas). Sometimes this question is appropriate and sometimes it's not. Where you do have responsibility today, however, is what you choose to do with the hurt and the anger, your relationship to the event today, whether you choose to forgive those who hurt you and move on, or whether you will keep rerunning the hurtful event in your mind for the rest of your life. After all, resentment derives from Latin word '*sentire*' meaning to 'to feel', so resentment means 'to re-feel'. Do you really want to keep re-feeling bitterness and animosity?

Resentment Reduction Question #2:
Where have I been a hypocrite?

This question is particularly useful if you feel you have a *justified resentment*. Justified resentment can be very tricky to get rid of, especially if we feel entitled to it. However, whether you have the right to be angry or not, staying angry will nevertheless feed your stress and bad habits. Perhaps someone might have been totally inconsiderate to you or wronged you. A question to ask yourself then is, 'Have I ever been inconsiderate in my life?' or 'Have I ever wronged anyone in my life?' Most of us probably have, at some point, even if to different extents. Yet, when we are angry, we can conveniently forget all of our shortcomings and become judgemental. For example, a prisoner might say, 'I might be a murderer, but at least I'm not a *paedophile*!' Likewise, a paedophile might say, 'I might be a paedophile, but at least I'm not a *murderer*!' Yet, aren't both as bad as one another in a sense, since they're both in prison?

Reminding yourself of your own shortcomings, however small, is a good way to get your ego off its high horse and move you one step closer towards serenity and freedom from resentment.

Resentment Reduction Question #3:
Is it possible this person was sick?

I once got angry with some fellows in recovery for being over-zealous, and so I mused to another fellow, 'Blimey, Twelve-Steps really is like a psychiatric ward at times!', to which she replied, 'The whole world's a psychiatric ward, hun.' Amen to that. One does not need to look very far to see that; every day, we see stories on the news about crime, violence, terrorism, corruption, scandals and so forth. On the internet, we see so much vitriol towards each other, for even the smallest infractions, such as liking (or disliking) a song. Want to start a row on the internet? Here's how:

1. Share an opinion.
2. Wait.

So, when you think of someone who has said or done something inconsiderate, I want you to picture this scenario: imagine you entered a psychiatric ward, and there was a seriously mentally unwell person in a hospital gown, mumbling gibberish to themselves. They then say something obnoxious to you, or something very unkind, and then they go back to sucking their thumb and perhaps yelling at the wall. Under ordinary circumstances, you might retaliate, and say something equally unkind in return. But this is a *sick* person. Surely you would treat them with compassion, patience and tolerance? Likewise, is it possible that whoever you are angry and frustrated with is sick, be it mentally, psychologically or spiritually? If so, how can you treat them with compassion?

Resentment Reduction Question #4:
What may have been going on for this person?

I once had a coachee, Jayne, come to a consultation thirty minutes late. I was fuming on the inside as I thought to myself, *She could've texted, emailed or called. How disrespectful of her! Who does she think she is?* As someone who has been abused a lot in the past, I'm very sensitive to any sign that someone doesn't respect me or my time. As she made her way upstairs to my consultation room, I began to rehearse in my head what I was going to tell her: 'So what are you here to work on? Is it your punctuality?' I couldn't wait to 'let her have it'. But for some reason, a little voice inside said to me: *Hear her out first.* So, I sat there and listened to her story. It turns out that on the way to her consultation, someone had collapsed at the Tube station. Jayne shared how she was a doctor, and given her profession, she felt duty called. She administered first aid and stayed with the poorly person until paramedics arrived to take them to hospital. And in that moment, I felt horrendously ashamed of myself. *How could have I been so judgemental?* I thought. And yet, how many of us are so quick to anger, but so slow to ask ourselves, 'What may be going on for this person?' Ever since, I've learned to give people the benefit of the doubt.

Likewise, with my noisy neighbour across the road; perhaps he had some trauma, and maybe blasting out music was his way of dealing with it. Perhaps the coronavirus lockdown had made him, like the rest of us, go a little bit stir-crazy because of having our need for autonomy and control, community and connection taken away. Again, I started to feel compassion. Sure, I felt a bit angry every time I heard the music, *but at least I didn't stay angry*. At least I connected to our common human-ity, instead of trying to go to a place of false moral superiority. Perhaps ancient wisdom about 'turn the other cheek' and for-giving over and over again is not such bad advice after all; we don't always have all the facts and the information, or the other side of the story.

Of course, two wrongs don't make a right. Just because you are in pain, it doesn't give you, or anyone else, a licence to hurt others. So instead of being just angry, see if you can be com-passionate, as this will lessen the anger; this will take you down from the place of self-righteous judgement. Think of this as being in the courtroom as a prosecutor, and then walking over to the other side of the court to hear the defence's arguments, and their mitigating circumstances. Once you've heard their side of the story, you might not be so harsh in judging. In real-life courts, judges do the same before deciding sentencing; they will hear what may mitigate the sentence, such as having a difficult childhood, mental health difficulties, and so forth. Perhaps you too can do the same. To quote executive coach Dr Marilee Adams: 'We're all recovering judgers.'

It's easy to think, *Well, I would* never *do what they have done*. But if you haven't done the same yet, perhaps it's because you haven't been hurt in the same way that they have. A great film I watched to demonstrate this was *The Shack* (based on the book by William P. Young). In it, the protagonist, Mack, meets a woman called Sophia, the personification of God's wisdom, who gives Mack the opportunity to be a judge. First, he is asked if he condemns his father, who beat him senseless in fits of alcoholic rage. Mack says, 'Of course, I condemn him!' Next, he is shown a clip of another young boy being beaten by his father, and is asked if he condemns him, to which he replies, 'No . . . he's just a little boy!' And Sophia says to him, 'That boy is *your father.*' And in that moment, Mack cries. Likewise, when I think of abusive relatives and some of the things that were done to me, I must remember that they suffered similarly, and worse things were done to them in some cases. The cycle of 'generational trauma' continues – unless we stop it by refusing to inflict what has been inflicted upon us.

Resentment Reduction Question #5:
Do I need to accept it or change it?

When something bothers us, we have three options:

1. Stay annoyed and angry at it.
2. Accept the way it is.
3. Change it.

You probably don't want to stay angry, especially if you are trying to abstain from your bad habit. So, you have to decide: do you need to accept it, or change it? To accept something means to stop resisting 'what is', so that your time and energy are freed up to be used more productively. Trying to change something that cannot be changed is a bit like being angry at the sun for being yellow and not purple. I mean, could you imagine saying, 'I'm angry because the sun isn't purple, and it should be!' You might as well sigh, accept how things are, and then move on. Case in point: when I was away on holiday once in Spain, I was sitting at a beach restaurant and to my annoyance, several people were smoking. *How inconsiderate!* I thought angrily. *It's bad enough they want to punish their lungs, but why should mine be punished too?* As they were polluting people's lungs with second-hand smoke, I became more and more irate, and then I asked myself, *What can I do about it?* Well, four options came to mind:

1. Do nothing and stay angry at them for being inconsiderate.
2. Accept it and try to put up with it.
3. Ask if they could stop smoking and risk making a scene and ruining the chilled beach vibes.
4. Accept it and leave the restaurant.

I tried Option 2, but I found myself coughing and seething on the inside. So, this left me with Option 3 or 4. Generally, my experience of asking people to stop smoking hasn't gone down well. It's most likely because people either feel shame for being asked to stop and feel they are being told off, or that their need for autonomy is being violated.

Begrudgingly, I went with Option 4. I was fuming and muttering to myself afterwards in my head. *Who do they think they are? I'll show them* ... But, looking back, it was probably the right thing to do. Why risk getting into an argument on holiday? Would it really be worth it? Some battles are simply not worth fighting. At times, it's far better for our own sanity to just accept that some people are inconsiderate, and that we cannot change or fix them or the situation.

Of course, there are times when we *can* make a change on a much more important level beyond petty annoyances such as second-hand cigarette smoke. For example, Martin Luther King Jr decided to use his anger at racial inequality in the United States to bring about change. He could have just grumbled, and smothered his feelings with ice cream, like I used to whenever I was frustrated. Instead, he chose to do something proactive: he started a civil rights movement, inspired mass peaceful protests and was a major driving force in creating laws that prevent discrimination on the grounds of race. *Remember that anger can always be transformed into creativity, positive action and change.*

Resentment Reduction Question #6:
What am I afraid of?

Often when we are angry, we are afraid of something, and anger is merely the protection mechanism. We may be afraid of being not worthy of love, appreciation or respect, or we may be afraid of being taken advantage of, or we may be afraid of our needs not being met. Thus, it's worth asking yourself, 'What am I afraid of?' and seeing if there is any fear behind the anger. For example, while driving, if someone cuts you up, you may be fearful for your or your family's physical safety, and thus anger or rage is your emotional brain trying to protect you.

Resentment Reduction Question #7:
What does this person need?

Asking this question while angry will probably not yield anything constructive and could lead to an answer along the lines of 'They need a good walloping!' But once we are calm, we can ask this with a clear head. Perhaps what they need is more consideration, self-awareness, honesty, personal growth, or healing. In coaching and psychotherapy, there's a model known as the Johari Window. In summary, it's a two-by-two grid, with 'Known to self' and 'Not known to self' on the x-axis, and on the y-axis, 'Known to others' and 'Not known to others'. There may be things others know about us, but we don't know – these are our blind spots. Is it possible your enemies also have theirs? In counselling, it's called 'Edge of Awareness', and sometimes, people's patterns and behaviours are outside their Edge of Awareness. Thus, if you cannot wish for their happiness, can you wish for their healing, growth or increased self-awareness as a fellow human being?

Whatever you think this person (or organisation) needs, how can you wish or hope that they receive it? For me, I find that sincerely praying for them and asking that they receive whatever it is they need in order to grow as a human being can work wonders for reducing my resentment towards them. It also helps me to remember that this person could be mentally or spiritually sick and it transforms my self-righteous anger to genuine compassion and love. You might prefer to do a loving-kindness meditation – it doesn't really matter, as long as you are sending them 'good vibes' in some way and wishing for their healing and growth.

Some of us may protest and say, 'No way, I'm not wishing *that* person well! They deserve everything coming!' If you're like me, you may even be *addicted* to resentments and afraid to forgive because you're scared of being a doormat or hurt again. But remember, if you have agreed to go to *any* lengths to recover, then this really is 'any lengths'. You're also not doing this for them; you're doing it for *you*. Keep in mind that every single one of us is flawed – and capable of redemption and growth. For example, one of my good friends used to be addicted to crack and prostitutes. He even *stole* from his parents to fund his habits. Now, he's a clean and sober psychotherapist who helps people with similar issues. A few coachees of mine have also done stints in prison and are now respected entrepreneurs. Clearly, criminals can reform and become valued members of society, who later regret their earlier behaviour. Finally, just because you forgive and wish your enemies well, it doesn't mean you have to be their best friend or keep them in your life; you can continue to keep boundaries. Next, let's take a look at resentment's cousin: *fear.*

GROWTH ACTION

Take an inventory of your resentments

1. Write out the following columns:

   – Who I resent
   – Why
   – Which parts of self were affected

Then complete the columns with your top ten resentments.

For example:
Who I resent: *My next-door neighbour*
Why: *They make a lot of noise. They don't clean up after their dog. They're not nice to me.*
Which parts of self were affected: *Serenity, personal relations, self-esteem.*

Now for each entry, apply one of the Resentment Reduction Questions in this chapter.

For example:
Where have I been a hypocrite? *I can also make a lot of noise with my children. I am also not nice to some people.*
What can I do about it? *I could move home if it's that bad. I could buy some noise-cancelling headphones. I could sound-insulate my property. I could try to accept 'what is'.*

> **Is it possible this person is sick?** Yes – when I asked them if they could turn down their music they violently threatened me!
>
> 2. Share this Resentment Inventory out loud with someone you trust to remove some of the emotional charge and get it off your chest, to feel reassured, and maybe even hear if there's another perspective that could reduce your resentment.

Running from fear

Fear is rife in us human beings. In fact, many of us carry an inherent *unconscious negative bias*: we can be biased towards expecting negative outcomes. Such negative bias is a survival mechanism, because we're less likely to die if we imagine the worst-case scenario and take action to prevent it. The problem with fear is that it gives bad habits more ammunition and makes them more enticing, since it would offer you a temporary reprieve from such fear and anxiety.

By taking a Fear Inventory, we shine a spotlight on what is making us anxious. When we stop to ask *why* we are so afraid, it helps to engage the more rational parts of our brain by getting the fear out of our head and on to paper. We can then share our Fear Inventory aloud with another person to get the same benefits as we did with sharing our Resentment Inventory.

To take a Fear Inventory, create a new table with four columns:

- What I am fearful of?
- Why?
- What this affects
- Fear reduction

Many of us also make decisions based on fear. Addictions like workaholism are very much a fear-based disease: a fear of not having enough, not doing enough and not being enough. Many people also use addictions and bad habits to numb feelings like anxiety, or at least to keep them at bay. I know when fear of financial insecurity takes hold of me, this is often a big driver for my workaholism, and I end up with the unconscious narrative: *I'll be safer if I work harder.* Sadly, working harder often just drives me into the ground and damages my health and sanity.

How can we reduce fear? There are a number of fear-reduction strategies – let's explore them:

Fear Reduction Question #1:
What's my part in creating this fear?

You might have a tendency to assume the worst-case scenario, or to view today's events from the conditioning you carry created from past events. You might be doing things to contribute to the fear. Take the fear of loss of financial security, for example. You could be contributing to this fear with poor personal finance decisions, such as taking on too much high-interest debt, gambling or spending too much on non-essentials. Or perhaps you have a tendency to catastrophise or jump to conclusions. After asking yourself this question numerous times for your fears, you may start to notice you engage in a certain pattern of thinking or behaving that contributes to the fear.

Fear Reduction Question #2:
How do I know for sure this will happen?

This is a question I sometimes ask my coachees, to which the answer, 99 per cent of the time, is: 'I don't.' If you don't know for certain, then why worry? *Many fears are simply projections of negative scenarios.* A great example of projected fears was the

'Y2K computer bug' hysteria, which happened just before the year 2000. This was because some computer systems would store four-digit years with only two digits. For example, 1998 would be stored as just 98 to save on computer memory. The problem with doing this, of course, is how does a computer system differentiate between the year 2000 and the year 1900? Both would be represented by 00. As a result, and fuelled by some hysterical headlines, many people believed that planes would fall out of the sky, nuclear reactors would malfunction, water and electricity supplies would fail, and civilisation itself would completely collapse. Thus, many started stockpiling food, and even building bunkers. In the end, well, not much happened. There were mostly minor disruptions, but certainly no apocalypse or 'digital doomsday' as predicted. An electronic sign in Nantes in France did however display the year '1900' on 3 January 2000 – *quelle catastrophe*! How did people ever cope with the fallout of such a Y2K blunder?

Have a think about whether you too might be committing a 'Y2K' fallacy. I also sometimes jokingly ask my clients, 'Do you have a crystal ball?' The answer is, of course, they don't. None of us can predict the future with total accuracy. And in a way, that's *exciting* – because tomorrow is full of endless possibilities.

Fear Reduction Question #3:
What can I do to right-size this fear?

When I was in recovery for dysfunctional relationships, a sponsor (a 12-Step Recovery coach) introduced me to the idea of *right-sizing* fears. For some time, I had a mostly irrational fear that I had undiagnosed HIV, despite the fact I wasn't into highly risky activities, such as sharing needles with heroin addicts, or having lots of unprotected sex. In any case, it was a fear that lingered, and any fear had the potential to make me turn back to bad habits to numb or soothe myself. Thus, my sponsor in recovery at the time asked me, 'Why don't you go and get an HIV test to find out for sure?' For some reason, the thought had never crossed my mind. Perhaps in my addicted brain, it was easier to keep doing my bad habits instead of addressing the underlying emotions and causes. Sure enough, I got tested, and the HIV test came back negative (as a part of me expected). That was one less fear to worry about, and as a result, it reduced the ammunition for my addictions.

Another fear I have also had is running out of money. One thing that a previous coach helped me to discover is that I find it reassuring to do a regular cashflow review and forecast: I look at what has been going out, how much has been coming in and how many months *financial runway* I have – how long can I operate my business for until I am out of cash. After doing this exercise, I found that I had more than enough to keep me going. So the fear that I will be bankrupt tomorrow if a client doesn't sign up is another irrational one and has no basis or merit! Thus, the fear again had been *right-sized*; the mountain had become a mere molehill.

Fear Reduction Question #4:
What will I do if this fear is true?

Much of this was covered in Chapter 2 when we explored setting up personal financial contingency plans. It can be a great question that can be applied to other contexts too, such as the fear of losing a job, or the fear of losing a partner. Remember that you tend to have more options than you think.

Fear Reduction Question #5:
Is this really true?

Sometimes there is a lie behind your fear. Perhaps that lie was put there by someone else – for example, the lie you may believe is 'I am not worthy'. One of the reasons you might believe this is because perhaps someone from your childhood abused you. Note that the definition of child abuse, according to internationally renowned childhood trauma and addiction recovery specialist Pia Mellody, is *anything less than nurturing behaviour towards a child*. I would also extend this to adults: *anything less than respectful behaviour is abuse*. Similarly, you might believe, 'I'm broke'. Is that really true? Perhaps you might be broke *this month*, but, on the whole, you still have a roof over your head, and perhaps *some* money in your bank account. Remember not to believe everything you think or feel! Some thoughts and feelings can be because of that silly amygdala again . . .

Fear Reduction Question #6:
Who can help me with this fear?

Sometimes, we need the help of someone else for various reasons. Firstly, when we are highly aroused, we cannot think clearly because the emotional brain has hijacked our thinking, so something as simple as talking to a person you trust can help you work through fears – and can be necessary. Other times we may need the help of a professional coach or therapist to overcome a fear, especially if it is connected to phobia or trauma. Have a think about who might be able to help you with this fear.

Fear Reduction Question #7:
How can I develop more faith?

I often ask my clients, 'What's the opposite of fear?' They tend to respond with words such as *courage*. However, courage is not quite the opposite, as one can still be very fearful in the act of doing something courageous, such as running into harm's way or risking one's life to save someone else. The opposite of fear is then not courage, but *faith*. For example, if I have *total* faith that the sun will rise tomorrow, then how could I possibly be fearful that the sun will not rise again? *Total faith cannot coexist with total fear.* Of course, faith can be a very personal matter, and will mean different things to different people. How you choose to develop more faith is entirely up to you. Some sort of spiritual faith, however, can certainly be beneficial, as we will explore later in Chapter 6. Next, we need to consider *guilt* – another lethal force behind addiction.

GROWTH ACTION

Take an inventory of your fears

1. Write out the following columns:

   – What/who I am fearful of?
   – Why?
   – Parts of self affected

Then complete the columns with your top ten fears.

For example:
Who/what I fear: *Running out of money.*
Why: *Because I spend recklessly. I overspend. My flat costs a lot of money.*
Which parts of self were affected: *Finances.*

Now for each fear, apply one of the Fear Reduction Questions in this chapter.

For example:
What will I do if this fear comes true? *I will ask my landlord for more time to pay the rent. I will seek professional financial*

> *advice about getting an overdraft if need be. I will stay with a*
> *friend for a while if I have to.*
> **What can I do to develop more faith?** *I will spend at least*
> *ten minutes a day visualising a more prosperous future.*
> **Who can help me with this fear?** *My coach, my counsellor, a*
> *financial adviser.*
>
> If you are struggling to think of fears you harbour, have a
> think about what keeps you awake at night or what you
> worry about the most.
>
> 2. Read this inventory out loud to someone you trust.

Running from guilt

'We are as sick as our secrets', is another classic saying from
12-Step. In other words, if we keep dark secrets, they will
keep us filled with fear, guilt and shame, and will erode our
self-esteem. There is much psychology literature pointing to
the connection between shame and addiction. What is 'guilt'?
Essentially, it's a feeling that you've done something wrong.
This can in some cases then lead to the equally destructive
feeling of *shame* ('I am wrong') and low self-esteem.

You may have done bad things, but that doesn't have to define
who you are. None of us are perfect – not even me, your beloved
life coach. There are people who I have hurt (ex-girlfriends in
particular) who I can't make amends to, because to do so would
injure them further. When we share our secrets, with trusted
and non-judgemental people, it takes the power out of them;
darkness is obliterated when it's brought into light. In some
cases, my confidantes, or people they knew, had done or had

experienced similar things, which made me feel less shameful and more 'normal'.

For your guilt inventory you will write four columns:

1. **Who did I hurt?**
2. **What I did to them**
3. **Where was I at fault?**
4. **Guilt reduction**

In Column 1 (Who did I hurt?), write the name of who you hurt. In Column 2 (What I did to them), be honest about what you did. In Column 3 (Where was I at fault?), you will write down 'I was . . .' followed by either selfish, self-seeking, inconsiderate, dishonest – or any other words of your choosing. Writing out the first three columns will be painful. But in Column 4 (Guilt reduction), you will apply one of the Guilt Reduction Questions which will wash some of the guilt away, restoring you to a sense of wholesomeness again.

Afterwards, you will write a list of your darkest and deepest secrets – and you will share this with a trusted person. This can be, at times, a very uncomfortable process, and you may feel more at ease telling a therapist or a professional coach. But when we share our darkest secrets and we find that people still respect and love us anyway, this can be very cathartic and healing.

Guilt Reduction Question #1:
What can I do to put this right without hurting others?

We cannot change the past, but we can make reparations. For example, not only can you say sorry, but you can ask the person, 'What can I do to put this right?' For example, perhaps you had an anger attack in a restaurant and broke something in a fit of rage. You could go back to the restaurant and not only apologise, but also pull out your wallet and ask if you can replace whatever you broke. But in some cases, apologising can hurt others: if you have ever cheated on someone, I would personally not recommend telling that person you had; it would most likely injure them further. Instead, you should probably make a *living amends* instead (see next question).

Guilt Reduction Question #2:
How can I make a living amends?

Sometimes we cannot make reparations or amends because it would injure others. For example, an ex-girlfriend was very firm about me not contacting her ever again as she was so hurt by me breaking her heart. As I respect her wishes, what I can do is make sure that I don't repeat the same mistakes again – also known as a *living amends* – a way to 'atone' or make up for that damage that cannot be fixed. For me, that would mean taking it very slow with my next partner, rather than rushing in at a thousand miles per hour only to suddenly decide that I'm with the wrong person.

Guilt Reduction Question #3:
What's my relationship to perfection here?

It's so easy to feel guilt over something you have done wrong. But remember what I said about Michael Jordan – one of the world's best basketball players? No matter how much he has practised, he *still* manages to make mistakes – which he openly admits. You too can let yourself off the hook for being less than perfect. Normally, those who struggle with shame have often internalised a story that they were somehow wrong as human beings for not being perfect.

Guilt Reduction Question #4:
What would I say to a friend who had made the same mistake?

For some reason, it can be easier to give compassion to someone who isn't us. Perhaps that's because it bypasses our ego. Perhaps because of low self-esteem, we can find it difficult to practise self-compassion. We can tell ourselves, 'I don't deserve this.' Thus, it can be easier instead to imagine if your best friend has made the same mistake as you. What would you say to them? I imagine you would probably give them some comforting words, and reassure them.

Guilt Reduction Question #5:
If I knew what I know now, would I have behaved differently?

All of us are doing the best that we can with the resources we have available at the time. Mistakes can therefore be learning opportunities, where there is no such thing as failure, only feedback. The feedback, of course, can be in the form of a rude awakening, whether it's a partner leaving us, losing a friend, or even getting a criminal conviction. I for one didn't know what unhealthy relationship patterns looked like (which I'll cover in the next chapter) until I had a string of break-ups and did some intensive work with a therapist. How could I have known before? You cannot change what you are not aware of. All I had seen or experienced growing up were my parents' relationships, and abusive relationships with my peers – none of which were positive role models. I didn't realise I had a problem, nor was I consciously aware about the patterns I was running. Carl Jung was right; the unconscious parts of ourselves make us run our lives on autopilot. We all have hidden programming and patterns, which until we become consciously aware of them dominate our lives without us knowing. Thus, I can forgive myself for not knowing any better. If you knew exactly what was going to happen, if you knew what you know now, then I suspect you would have behaved differently. If you knew just how severe the consequences would be for you or for others, then I suspect you might have chosen differently.

Guilt Reduction Question #6:
What could *have I done instead?*

When we use the phrase, 'I should have done [xyz]', or 'I should have known better', we are shaming ourselves for not having mastered life. 'Should' leads to *shame*:

SHAME = Should Have Already Mastered Everything

'*Could*', however, reframes expectations of perfection into possibilities and alternatives. Thus, avoid using the phrase 'I *should* have', for example, 'I should have not done that'. Instead, use the phrase 'I *could* have'. This removes the expectation of yourself to be perfect. You *could* stop using 'should'!

If you are struggling with addiction, then it could be time to seek some additional help.

GROWTH ACTION

Take a guilt inventory

I. Write out the following columns:

– Who have I hurt or what have I kept secret?
– Why?
– Parts of self affected

Then complete the columns with your guilt.

For example:
What I have kept secret: *Reading my partner's emails and texts to see if they are cheating.*
Why: *I am scared that I am not good enough and that they will leave me.*
Which parts of self were affected: *Self-esteem, personal relations.*

Now for each entry, apply one of the Guilt Reduction Questions in this chapter.

For example:
What can I do to make a living amends? *I can't tell my partner as it will injure them, but I will stop doing this immediately and get help for my low self-esteem and overly suspicious behaviour.*

If you are struggling to think of guilt you harbour, think about something you've done which you wouldn't want your family, friends, colleagues, or boss to know about.

2. What deep and dark secrets do you have? Write them down.
3. Now share this inventory with someone who you really trust and read it aloud to them.

Getting help

When I was about eight years old, my father took me to a water park where there were some artificial currents which you could ride in inflatable rings. I was enjoying myself in the shallow end, when suddenly, I felt myself get pulled into the deep end, and before I knew it, I was being swept away by the current. As a child who couldn't swim well, it was terrifying to be caught in one. The harder I tried to get out, the more I struggled; I felt utterly helpless. Luckily, I could see a lifeguard and so I began frantically waving my hands at him. Upon seeing I was in trouble, he quickly grabbed a pole and offered me it, which I grabbed on to and was pulled to safety. If it weren't for him, I could have been in deep trouble. Sometimes, it's dangerous to go alone. Our emotions are like those currents. When we are happy, it can be pretty easy to stay abstinent from our choice of vice. But when life gets rocky, uncomfortable or challenging, those waves of emotion can be pretty big, disorientating and very hard to surf! And if we don't have enough support, we'll be pushed into a direction where we take refuge in bad habits.

Furthermore, sometimes trying to use willpower alone to recover from addiction is like trying to move a broken-down car up a hill by pushing it with your own strength, without ever stopping to pop open the hood and inspect the engine and see *why* it has stopped working. If your car broke down, you would probably call someone more experienced in cars, such as a mechanic or breakdown recovery service, and have them take a look and point out what's going on. For example, you may engage in certain behavioural, thinking or emotional patterns that ultimately make you more likely to relapse. In other words, you may benefit from seeking outside help, from someone more experienced or knowledgeable, instead of trying to go it totally alone and trying to travel in that broken-down car of your life alone.

Of course, the questions and exercises in this book may bring you enough clarity to break your bad habit, in which case, you need not do anything more except to stay vigilant that you don't slip back into the old habit! However, if you find that you're still struggling to stop, then it may be time to seek out a recovery group as well as a professional coach or therapist. In the Appendix there is a list of recovery groups should you wish to pursue this as an option.

In a nutshell

Addictions and bad habits are synonymous, except many of us feel more comfortable with the latter term, as 'addiction' sounds a bit extreme and has very negative connotations to many: *Me? Addicted? No way.*

However, an addiction is simply the continued behaviour of using of a substance or a process despite negative consequences. Thus, given how many bad habits exist, one has to ask if we are kidding ourselves when we say, 'I'm not addicted, I've just got a bad habit.' Deep down, you know which behaviours are making your life unmanageable, even if it's a little bit. Perhaps it's caused arguments with your partner, maybe you've under-performed at work as a result, perhaps your weight yo-yos, or maybe your finances are somewhat affected. Sometimes it's not until the consequences are so severe that we *finally* admit we have a problem. The hardest thing to do can be to admit that you have a problem and that you need some help nipping it in the bud. But if you have done this, then congratulations: you are on your way to beating that 'bad habit' one day at a time! The next step is examining what you are running from and why, whether it's unmet needs, fear, resentment or shame, and what can you do about it – or, at least, can you change your perspective on it and thus reduce it?

From my experience, having an addiction is like having a lake of stagnant water; our addictive way of thinking keeps us stuck, and so we need to continually let the old way of thinking flow out and allow the fresh water of new ideas, perspectives and ways of being to come into our being. As we hear what the voices of addiction and the voices of recovery sound like, we become more consciously aware of how to make better and healthier choices. It's also good to be reminded of what the consequences of using are as well as what the promises of recovery are, and thus, a good recovery meeting is one that incorporates both sharing of woes as well as experience, strength and hope of recovery.

So instead of picking up a beer or a pint of ice cream (or whatever your preferred 'bad habit' is), pick up the phone. Connect. As connection really is the opposite of addiction. It's not only sanity that is a group activity; *addiction recovery is also a group activity*. It doesn't have to be a 12-Step group – it could be a friend or another group. And remember to avoid being HALT: Hungry, Angry, Lonely or Tired.

In this chapter, we learned about some of the major unconscious forces in our psyche that can drive our bad habits, as well as how to reduce such forces. It's also important to consider the unconscious forces such as underlying motivations that can drive our behaviours and our relationships with others, which we'll explore in the next chapter.

CHAPTER 4

What's My Hidden Motivation?

'Until you make the unconscious conscious, it
will direct your life, and you will call it "fate".'

—CARL JUNG

In this chapter, we will explore hidden motivations. By motivation, I don't mean life purpose (that will come later in
Chapters 5 and 6), but I mean the real reason why you want
to do what you want to do, and what unconsciously drives the
majority of your actions.

Most of us have an overriding unconscious motivation behind
most of our actions and goals. When you understand and uncover
what your deepest motivation is, you can then also uncover
really useful other information, such as your emotional triggers,
strengths, weaknesses and blind spots, as well as how to develop
your character so that you become more balanced. And one
fantastic tool for discovering these unconscious motivations is
the *Enneagram*.

The hidden motivation dominating your life

Introducing the Enneagram

To put it simply, the *Enneagram* is an ancient system for developing one's character consisting of nine interconnected personality types. Its name comes from Greek: *'ennea'* meaning nine, and *'gramma'* meaning something that's drawn or written down. Its original source has been contested, but some scholars and historians believe it can be traced back to ancient Judaism, Sufism, and the Christian Desert Fathers. It was brought back into mainstream psychology and personal development by the philosopher Oscar Ichazo and psychiatrist Claudio Naranjo in the 1970s. It is now used by coaches and psychotherapists to assist them in understanding their clients' deepest motivations. There are nine different character types in the Enneagram, which are separated not by behaviour, but by *motivation*. For instance, two Enneagram types can exhibit the same behaviour but may have two totally different motivations as to *why* they are doing it – and that's what makes this system unique.

The Enneagram is also different to other personality typing systems in that it is not designed to box us into static archetypes, but rather, to reveal to us what boxes we have unconsciously already put ourselves in, and what we need to do in order to break out of that box. It should also be noted that one can resonate with several different types in different amounts. Often, we have a primary motivation, followed by a secondary one (known as a 'wing').

The nine Enneagram types

Broadly speaking, here are what the nine different Enneagram types are motivated by, as well as their main vices, and some key questions each type needs to ask their self:

Type 1 – The Perfectionist ('I need to be perfect')

The Perfectionist feels compelled to do the right thing and 'be perfect', as they believe the world is imperfect. As a result of this motivation, they can be very diligent, detail-oriented but also very puritanical, judgemental and inflexible at times. As a result, their main vice is *anger* – but it's often felt internally and not expressed because to express it would be to appear 'less than perfect'. When triggered by imperfection in themselves, they need to coach themselves by asking, 'How is chasing perfection making things more imperfect?' and 'How is not feeling perfect enough making me angry at myself?' When triggered by imperfection in others, they may also need to ask themselves, 'Where have I been a hypocrite?', so as to reduce judgemental anger towards others (as we covered in the Running from Resentments section of the previous chapter).

Type 2 – The Helper ('I need to be appreciated and needed')

The Helper has a core motivation to be helpful and to be needed. Their core story is 'I'm only worthy if I am appreciated and needed.' As a result of this motivation, they can be very flattering and giving, but it can be done with *covert contracts* (i.e. 'I'm doing this with the expectation that you'll love and appreciate me'), and sometimes it can be very manipulative. They often care too much about what others think, thus their main vice is *pride* – they just want to know they are loved by others. Feeling taken for granted and unappreciated can be triggering for them, thus, they need to reflect and ask themselves, 'Why do I feel the need to be appreciated so much?'

Type 3 – The Competitive Achiever ('I need to be the best')

The Achiever is driven to be the best. The story they create is 'I need to be a winner or I'm not worthy.' As a result, they can be very driven, competitive, but also impatient, and at their worst, deceitful. Their main vice is *vanity* – because they are so concerned about *appearing* as if they are successful and winning. Someone making them look bad professionally can be a trigger for their anger. They often overcompensate for a lack of self-worth with overachieving. Questions Type 3s need to repeatedly ask themselves include 'How do I try to make myself feel more valuable?' and 'Why is appearing successful so important to me?'

Type 4 – The Individualist ('I need to be special and unique')

The Individualist longs to be special, unique and different and find their identity. They are driven by a story of 'As long as I am special, unique, and not ordinary, then I am worthy.' They can be very authentic and very in touch with themselves, and many Type 4s can become extraordinary creative artists who really stand out. However, their main vice is *envy*; they do not like other people being recognised for their specialness (which they may feel will threaten the amount of love and attention they will receive). They also hate being ignored (because that would mean they are ordinary!). In addition, Type 4s are well known for suffering from *melancholy* and *self-pity*; they can have quite a sad view of life, one that ignores the goodness around them or in front of them. A question to help them overcome their envy is 'What's the story I create when I feel I could be missing out?' Another question they can ask to overcome their melancholy is 'What am I grateful for?' and 'Who can I serve?'

to overcome self-pity (refer to the need for 'Selfish v. Service Mode' in Chapter 5 about why this helps).

Type 5 – The Specialist ('I need to understand')

The Specialist wants to deeply understand and to acquire vast knowledge. The story they tell themselves is 'As long as I understand, I will be OK. I must conserve resources and gather knowledge.' As a result, they can be very studious, observant, detailed, but they can also be quite aloof, detached and overly intellectual. Their main vice is *stinginess* with their time or energy, which is often as a result of spending too much time and energy thinking and analysing (they live a lot 'in their head'). Given their overactive thinking, they can feel easily overwhelmed by the demands of others or perhaps by people who talk a lot. A contemplative question they need to ask themselves is 'Why do I believe I have limited energy to deal with the unexpected?'

Type 6 – The Sceptic ('I need to keep myself safe')

The Sceptic is motivated by being safe and belonging. The story they have created is 'I must keep myself safe as the world is a dangerous place.' Thus, they can be very good at spotting potential risks, planning for the worst, as well as being loyal to those who they have vetted as trustworthy. However, as a result of their story, they can be very sceptical and anxious. The vice they suffer from the most is thus *fear*. The questions they need to ask themselves are 'Why am I paralysed by my projections?' and 'How can I develop more faith?'

Type 7 – The Visionary ('I need to experience it all')

The Visionary is enticed by a desire to experience it all. Their core story is 'I need to experience everything, the world is full of possibilities, and as long as I experience excitement, I can avoid pain.' Because of this motivation, they can be great at spotting opportunities, they can be visionaries and see limitless potential in life. Unfortunately, wanting to experience it all leads to the vice of *gluttony* – a greed for more experiences (rather than food). Often this wanting more is to avoid some kind of pain or discomfort, which can lead them to avoiding their commitments. Therefore, the question they need to ask themselves is 'What am I running from through fantasy or escapism?' (Refer also back to Chapter 3.)

Type 8 – The Challenger ('I need to be strong and in control')

The Challenger is motivated by being strong and being in control. Their story is 'I must not be weak, I must be independent and in control; the world is a harsh place where only the strong survive.' This Enneagram type thus doesn't have a problem speaking up, saying what they feel needs to be said, and challenging those who they feel need to be challenged. However, their vice is *lust* – for more power and control. Their triggers are thus being controlled and injustice. In addition, being perceived as weak in any way can also trigger this type. The questions they need to ask themselves are 'What am I scared of when I'm not getting my way?' and also, 'How do I try to be strong?'

Type 9 – The Peacemaker ('I need to keep the peace')

The Peacemaker simply wishes to maintain harmony and avoid conflict. The story they tell themselves is 'I am OK as long as others around me are OK – everyone needs to be heard and respected.' As a result, they can be very accommodating and often 'go with the flow'. However, someone being disrespectful can trigger quite explosive anger from them, especially as they tend to bottle up their frustration and feelings! Their main vice is *sloth* – a kind of disengagement from themselves; they can be great at accommodating everyone else except themselves. When triggered by conflict, the question they need to ask themselves is 'What disharmony do I create by not speaking up for myself?'

Motivation – not behaviour

After reading these types, it's totally normal to see yourself to some extent in all of them, and we often resonate with each of the nine different motivations in varying amounts. Remember though: what separates the Enneagram types isn't behaviour – it's the *underlying motivation*. Which motivation did you resonate with the most? Often there is one core motivation that we tend to be drawn towards more than any of the others, and this core motivation tends to be fixed – our main Enneagram type doesn't change. However, what can change is our overall awareness of the type as well as its shadow side. There is a multiple-choice comprehensive assessment you can do online to more accurately determine your core Enneagram type, visit nickhatter.com/enneagram for more information.

Counter-types

If you didn't resonate particularly with any one motivation, it might be because you are either not consciously aware of what your truest motivation is, or in some cases, you may not be totally honest with yourself. Another explanation could be that you may be what is known in the Enneagram as a 'counter-type', i.e. you actively try to go against the grain of your instinct or core motivation. For example, here are the counter-types of the Enneagram:

- **Type 1:** openly expresses anger rather trying to contain it in a perfectionistic way
- **Type 2:** wants to be taken care of but resists being dependent on others
- **Type 3:** has a vanity *for not having vanity* – they don't want people to know that they care about how they look to others and value modesty

- **Type 4:** is long-suffering and hides pain, whereas ordinary Type 4s tend to openly express it
- **Type 5:** is in touch with their emotions, but hides them
- **Type 6:** tries to overcompensate fear with action to prove they're not scared (known as 'counter-phobic')
- **Type 7:** is a glutton for service and self-denial rather than pleasure
- **Type 8:** looks out for the protection of the group rather than themselves
- **Type 9:** often have very full lives, but do not know who they truly are or what they want deep down

Remember: the Enneagram is not about behaviour, but *motivation*. Case in point: my Enneagram trainers, as an exercise, asked our cohort to guess their Enneagram types. We were absolutely *certain* we had the right answers; 'She's a Type 2 (Helper), and she's a Type 8 (Challenger). Easy!' However, we were all floored (and humbled!) when in fact, one of them was Type 4 (Individualist) and one of them was Type 3 (Competitive Achiever). The point the trainers were making was that determining someone's type on external behaviour is the wrong thing to do in the Enneagram. Ultimately, only the person knows deep down what their truest and deepest motivation is for why they do what they do. And likewise, the same goes for you. Thus, any websites that claim to know the primary Enneagram type of celebrities or well-known figures (without having done an in-depth Enneagram assessment with them) are inherently *wrong*, because most likely they are basing their typing on behaviour and not underlying motivation. Therefore, one can only speculate.

Another key thing to remember is this: *you are not your type.* Once you find out which Enneagram type you resonate with, do not start saying 'I am a type x' (as I explained in Chapter 1 in relation to mental health conditions, there's negative consequences of doing this). The Enneagram is not designed to be used this way.

Rather, it is to help you to understand what your ego has latched on to in order to feel safe or OK in the world, and the Enneagram is there to help you grow away from that fixation so that you can be more your authentic self and become more balanced and whole as a character. So instead, you can say 'I resonate with type x.'

When you discover which type (or which motivation) you resonate with most, you can then start to explore both the trigger and growth questions. Generally speaking, your core Enneagram type doesn't change, but your level of awareness can. Rather than blindly being driven by your unconscious motivations and triggers, you can start to bring them to conscious awareness. Then, you can choose to behave differently, rather than letting them run your life on autopilot and leaving you bewildered as to why you behaved that way or ended up in a particular state or situation.

GROWTH ACTION

Find your hidden motivations in life

1. Reflect on the following:

    i)   Which Enneagram motivations do you resonate with most?

    ii) Which self-coaching questions do you need to start using more often?

    iii) Which vices do you suffer from most?

    iv) How can you start to become more balanced in your character?

2. Find out your Enneagram type at nickhatter.com/enneagram

The hidden motivation in your relationships

When it comes to dating, relationships and friendships, we must be mindful of the following unconscious motivations and patterns that can create unhealthy relationships.

Love Avoidance ('I can't say no', 'I'm scared you'll hurt me')

Love Avoidance, in a nutshell, is where you're initially very seductive in a relationship. However, once the person starts to draw closer and naturally want more intimacy, you begin to pull away – perhaps by avoiding them or by being resentful and feeling 'trapped'. Eventually, the other person notices you are not emotionally available, and they may decide to pull away themselves. This, however, can then trigger feelings of abandonment and loneliness, so you decide to, in a last-minute scramble, see if you can get them to stay – perhaps by being seductive again. Being seductive doesn't necessarily mean sexually, although it can include that. Rather, seduction can mean telling the person what they want to hear, or perhaps making big gestures such as proposing to them. The cycle of Love Avoidance madness often starts with the following unconscious motivations:

- I must date this person as they are the best I can do
- I can't say 'no' to this person's love
- I don't want to be my own, but I don't really fancy them
- This person looks good on paper and I *should* like them
- I want love/sex, but I don't want a relationship with them

As a sponsor in recovery once taught me: *when dating, you want to turn down the intensity from eleven to one.* This means *definitely* no sex after just a couple of dates! Really take your time and get to know the person and slow down. Ask yourself:

- Do I really like them, or am I just looking for a reprieve from loneliness or any stressors in my life?
- Am I really attracted to them, or do I think I *should* be – do they just 'look good on paper'?
- Am I scared that this will be my last shot at love?

Attraction is not something that can be forced. It can develop over time (another reason to take things really slow), but you can't *think* your way into loving someone romantically, as I learned the hard way and only after many failed relationships. Just because they're a good person, stable and physically attractive, it still doesn't mean you can force feelings of romantic attraction towards them.

I used to think those who waited until marriage for sex (or at least, serious commitment) were prudes. But having experienced my own fair share of failed relationships, maybe they aren't so unwise after all. As one of my mentors taught me: *sex is like a nuclear reaction*; it needs to be contained with a solid foundation in order to be safe, or else there's going to be dangerous fallout. Often in our casual sex culture in the West (especially the UK and the US) we typically have sex first, *then* ask questions later (known as '*the* talk'). For instance, a comprehensive review of casual sex studies found that between 60 and 80 per cent of undergraduate university students had engaged in some sort of 'hook-up experience' (sexual activity outside of dating or a relationship).* In addition, Ashley Madison, a dating website

---

* J. R. Garcia, C. Reiber, S. G. Massey and A. M. Merriwether, 'Sexual Hookup Culture: A Review', *Review of General Psychology*, 16: 2 (2012), 161–176. https:// doi.org/10.1037/a0027911.

for married people actively seeking affairs, boasted 70 million users in 2020.* That's a lot of affairs! Furthermore, an analysis of the 174 songs that made it into the top ten in Country, Pop and R&B charts in the US, found that around 92 per cent of songs contained one or more 'reproductive messages' (mentions of sex), with an average of 10.49 phrases per song.† Is Western culture and art representative of society's feelings around hooking up?

Let's face it: our approach to sex as a society has become highly dysfunctional. We ought to get to know one another intimately, build deep trust and establish expectations, *before* getting sexual. This would then lead to far fewer disastrous relationships. It would give us all more time to really think about how we truly feel about a person, as well as agree expectations and boundaries, thus minimising confusion and reducing the risk of unrequited feelings. If you're lonely, and feeling desperate to have *anyone*, remember this: it's better to be unhappily single than unhappily married. I have too often seen people distressed by feeling trapped in bad relationships, or by acrimonious divorces.

Another form of unconscious motivation that manifests as Love Avoidance could be 'I want to be in a relationship, but I'm terrified of getting hurt.' This could be because of *trauma*; perhaps a parent abandoned you as a child, or maybe you have been in an abusive relationship, or suffered a bereavement. You may have had a parent or guardian who was overbearing, smothering, overshared, used you to satisfy their needs (known as *enmeshment*), or perhaps maybe even abused you emotionally, physically

---

* Dean Takahashi, 'Ashley Madison "married dating" site grew to 70 million users in 2020', VentureBeat – https://venturebeat.com/2021/02/25/ashley-madison-married-dating-site-grew-to-70-million-users-in-2020/ – accessed 31 March 2021.
† D. R. Hobbs and G. G. Gallup, 'Songs as a medium for embedded reproductive messages', *Evolutionary Psychology: An International Journal of Evolutionary Approaches to Psychology and Behavior*, 9:3 (2011), 390–416. https://pubmed.ncbi.nlm.nih.gov/22947982/.

or sexually. As a result, you may have developed a phobia of intimacy, connection and commitment. Unconsciously, you may have associated love with danger. In this case, you may find you need to seek professional help alongside your own personal development.

Love Addiction ('I *need* them')

Love Addiction can be characterised by a lot of neediness – often to someone who is abusive or unavailable. Many Hollywood films glamourise this dynamic (think of the protagonist who exclaims, 'I just can't live without you and I *need* you!'). It's viewing another person as more of a panacea for life's pains and low self-esteem, rather than as a human being. As love addiction expert Pia Mellody explains, it often starts with being attracted to the power or seduction of someone else, and then there's a 'high' as a *love fantasy* is triggered.* The person with Love Addiction experiences relief from the pain they are facing in their life (such as low self-esteem and unmet needs – refer back to Chapter 2). However, they deny the reality that the person is not available to them, thus they live in the fantasy of being in a relationship with that person. If someone is love addicted in a relationship, they may become more needy, and oblivious to the fact that their partner may not actually be available (people with love addiction can often end up dating people with Love Avoidance). Eventually, the person with Love Addiction starts to realise their love object is not available, the fantasy collapses, and then they may enter withdrawal, which is when they may obsess over how to get their love object back, get even, or attempt to find someone else to perhaps cover over the last hurt.

One of my clients, Veronica, was a leading coach from

---

* Pia Mellody, *Facing Love Addiction: Giving Yourself the Power to Change the Way You Love* (HarperCollins, 2003), 69.

Slovakia, a fit woman in her forties, with a very happy and positive personality. Things were mostly going fine in her life – except her relationship with her boyfriend, who told her, 'You're too *positive*. I don't like it.' He was becoming increasingly critical of her and he had become more distant. I told Veronica, 'It sounds like he doesn't really like you for who you are. I'm wondering what's making you stay with a man like him?' She said she loved him. 'But I wonder if he feels the same way, given what you've said.' She started crying; reality had finally hit home. 'I don't think he does.' Soon after our conversation, Veronica broke up with her boyfriend. But by our next session, she came back happy and excited. 'He completely changed. He begged me to stay, he took me out for dinner to a really expensive restaurant, he even bought me a lovely ring!' However, I wasn't convinced one bit. I explained to Veronica about the patterns of Love Addiction and Avoidance. And I was confident that her boyfriend was going through his abandonment trauma; he didn't want to be on his own, but he didn't want to be with *her*. So, I told Veronica, 'Unless he's done some serious work on himself, he will most likely go back to his old ways of being very critical of you.' And sure enough, that's *exactly* what happened. Within a few weeks, he was back to being miserable and critical of Veronica. He even asked for his ring back. Naturally, Veronica told him where he could stick that ring. Good for her! Thankfully, Veronica was finally able to see the pattern of Love Avoidance and Love Addiction and break free of it – because she had finally realised what was going on unconsciously; she was no longer sleepwalking into fate.

The Co-Dependent ('I can fix them!')

A co-dependent is, broadly speaking, someone who attempts to fix, manage, control or enable another's addictive or dysfunctional behaviour. This can be damaging for both the co-dependent and the person they're trying to fix. The co-dependent becomes increasingly frustrated and despairing as they try to (and fail to) fix the person with addiction or dysfunction. Unfortunately, I have fallen into this very pattern myself with an old friend of mine, Lawrence, who suffered from depression and post-traumatic stress disorder. Like me, he had a lot of childhood trauma and abuse. He was also living on benefits, as was I. So, in a lot of ways, I felt we were both in the same boat. I did all I could to help him. I took him to the Samaritans walk-in centre to see a counsellor, convinced my therapist to see him for a free session, brought him along to a 12-Step support group, loaned him various books on trauma recovery and listened to him complain endlessly about his girlfriend and his problems. I don't think I could have done more.

Like many people with co-dependency, I became increasingly frustrated because Lawrence wasn't getting any better. Nothing I did seemed to make any difference or be good enough for him. For example, the Samaritans weren't any good because 'they weren't psychologists', 12-Step wasn't any good because 'there were too many people complaining', my therapist wasn't good enough, and so forth. To make matters worse, when we would hang out, I started to feel increasingly drained of energy and tired. I didn't realise what was going on until later: he was sucking the life out of me. Eventually, my therapist had to say to me, 'Nick, stop trying to fix Lawrence. He can't be saved.' He was right. I was giving too much of myself to him. Eventually, I had to cut Lawrence out of my life.

Be really honest and ask yourself whether there's been any people you've decided to make into your 'project'. Have there been any people in your life who had serious addictive or dysfunctional behaviour, but you thought, *I can fix/change them*? If you try to change people free of charge, you're most likely co-dependent, but if you get paid to do it, then you're either a coach or a therapist! And even then, we professionals need to

be careful that we don't take too much responsibility for helping people change. Researchers estimate that around 40 per
cent of therapeutic and coaching outcomes is down to *external
factors* – things that happen outside of sessions and are beyond
the practitioner's control.*

Finally, you may not have the right skills and know-how to
help those closest to you, and even if you did, you are the wrong
person to help them as you have too much personal history with
them. They are better off being referred to a helping professional such as a life coach or a therapist.

The Needy Child ('I need their approval')

This has been a motivation trap I have fallen into myself. At
its root is a form of low self-esteem; *I don't feel worthy enough,
therefore, I need you to reassure me that I am OK.* You may find
yourself unconsciously feeling like a child around certain
people – especially people you deem to be an authority figure.
When we are being dominated by this motivation, we may
become people pleasers, say 'yes' when we want to say 'no',
and any form of criticism (perceived or actual) from them may
hurt extra deeply. I once had a therapist who, though he was
very good, would make me feel awful for days after he gave
me any negative feedback. At first, I had no idea why, until
one day it dawned on me: we had a child–parent relationship
dynamic. I realised I really revered him, and that I looked
up to him too much as a father figure. I took a lot of what
he said as gospel and I was afraid to disagree or speak up for
myself. Once I realised this dynamic, I pointed it out to him.
Unfortunately, despite bringing his conscious awareness to it,

---

* Douglas McKenna and Sandra Davis, 'Hidden in Plain Sight: The Active
Ingredients of Executive Coaching', *Industrial and Organizational Psychology*, 2
(2009), 244–260. https://dx.doi.org/10.1111/j.1754-9434.2009.01143.x.

the dynamic I felt didn't change. I was still getting triggered by him and still feeling like a child around him. In the end, I suggested that we end the therapeutic relationship. For this reason, I try to make sure that my coachees don't ever put me up on a pedestal, and I do my best to not be their guru/master/teacher, but rather, simply an equal and a facilitator. My coachees in fact often find my openness about sharing my faults, my past mistakes and my own shortcomings quite refreshing compared to other helping professionals who can be much more guarded.

Sometimes, you too may need to walk away from a relationship if you find you are unable to break the child–parent dynamic – and that's OK. Some people will bring the worst out in us, because your relationship with them matches the pattern of previous trauma – the person or their behaviour reminds you of someone who really hurt you (psychoanalysts call this *transference*). Sometimes it is far easier and less painful for both parties to walk away and detach with love.

Note that some of us can subtly and unconsciously need to feel like we are bigger or better than somebody else. This can in some cases turn us into a critical parent figure. A few times, in my life, I have had former friends and coaches decide it was their place to 'parent' me. Pay attention if you notice people around you being overly critical. Ask yourself, 'Is this what a critical parent might say?' and 'How old do I feel around this person?' If you feel quite young around the person, there's a good chance it's a child–parent relationship. In addition, the other person may not be consciously aware that they are co-creating a toxic child–parent relationship. Thus, it may be worth pointing out that perhaps you do not feel like they are speaking to you like an adult.

The Hero Child ('I can save my family!')

We can also be motivated deep down by wanting to save and rescue our dysfunctional family (known as the 'Hero Child' in psychotherapy circles). This is, however, a fool's errand. Saving and rescuing your family might look like, for example, over-achieving and workaholism, with the intent of somehow restoring the family's honour or image, with perhaps the unconscious belief that it would make you more worthy and lovable. From my own personal experience, being successful doesn't necessarily mean you will get the love and attention that you might crave deep down. And if you suddenly do, you have to ask yourself if it's real love, or if they're just trying to piggyback off your success. Do they love you for *who* you are, or *what* you have? Speaking of suc-cess, let's next have a look at your goals, and why you *really* want to achieve them. Note that there are more unconscious dysfunc-tional relationship patterns than the ones listed in this chapter.*

GROWTH ACTION

Reflect on the motivations in your relationships

Reflect on the following:

    i) Have you seen any of the above patterns play out in your relationships (past or present)?

    ii) If so, what motivated this?

    iii) What are/were the consequences of this?

What alternative choices could you make?

---

* Recommended further reading: *Games People Play: The Psychology of Human Relationships* by Eric Berne.

The hidden motivation behind your goals

One of my clients, Albert, was an extremely successful banker who was paid £1 million a year. When he sought me out, he had only one goal: to reach £2 million a year. I don't typically take on clients if I feel they only want to work with me to be rich (it just doesn't appeal to me much), but I liked Albert on a personal level and I felt a good connection, so I made an exception for him. From my coaching training, one of the things I learned was to 'find the goal behind the goal'. Now, a lot of coaches might have dived right in and helped him work towards this goal. After all, coaching is all about achieving goals, right? Well, not necessarily. Yes, it can be very goal- and outcome-focused, but it can include self-discovery and personal growth. So, I asked Albert, 'Tell me, if you made £2 million a year, what would this give you?' to which he replied, 'Hmm, a sense of satisfaction, I guess. And more financial freedom.'

Finding the 'goal behind the goal'

I have no issue with anyone wanting to make more money, or improve their life, but I couldn't help but feel somehow, at Albert's renumeration level, going from £1 million to £2 million a year wouldn't make that much of a difference to his quality of life – at least, not according to psychology studies. In 2010, the psychologist Daniel Kahneman and economist Sir Angus Deaton examined 450,000 well-being survey responses from 1,000 residents in the US. In their research, they found that earning over $75,000 (£66,487 in 2021) a year makes a negligible

difference to happiness levels.* Not at all surprising; money
can afford you many things, such as a nice house, or a nice car,
but financial security doesn't guarantee that you'll have true
friends, a community where you belong, healthy relationships or
meaning and purpose. During our sessions, Albert mentioned in
passing that he didn't like going home as he was having issues
with his wife. 'It sounds like the relationship at home with
your wife isn't that great. I'm wondering if you're using work
to escape?' Albert admitted this was the case, but he was too
afraid to do anything about it; he didn't want to be on his own
but neither did he want to necessarily be with his wife (note the
Love Avoidance motivation operating here, described earlier in
this chapter). Thus, Albert chose his goal for the wrong reasons.
So instead of working with Albert on his original money goal,
I worked with him on his marriage, and whether or not he was
in it for the right reasons, and he was able to get more clarity.
More money would not have solved his problems. What he was
actually looking for was time away from his wife.

Similarly, one of my clients, Catherine, was a successful entrepreneur who wanted to go from making eight figures to nine
figures a year in her business. Of course, I want to encourage
my clients to reach their full potential, and with this particular
client, she had contracted me to focus mostly on performance
coaching. Catherine told me that she needed to delegate and
entrust tasks more so that she could scale up operations. So, we
explored what threats there were to achieving her objectives.
One of them was *indecision*, which was due to difficulty trusting
others. When we explored why that was the case, we discovered
that Catherine had a fear of things going wrong and not living
up to *her* standard, looking bad and proving her incompetency

---

* Daniel Kahneman and Angus Deaton 'High income improves evaluation
of life but not emotional well-being', *Proceedings of the National Academy of
Sciences*, 107:38 (September 2010), 16489–16493; DOI: http://dx.doi.org/10.1073/
pnas.1011492107

(note that she was a strong Type 3 – Achiever – and thus, she was very image conscious). When I asked *who* she would be looking bad to, she thought about it, and then said, 'Myself, I guess.' So, we explored *why* she felt the need to prove it to herself, and it came back to her teenage years, where she felt she had developed a void of sorts. During those years, she felt empty, and that she didn't have health, wealth or love, and that she wasn't living up to her full potential. Ever since then, she felt that she needed to 'prove herself'. I observed that her image consciousness was in fact holding her back today from achieving the success she wanted; by being so concerned about how she perceived herself, this would, in her words, make her a bit of a 'control freak'. As a result of not being able to let go of control, she would end up micromanaging, and taking on lower-value tasks, rather than high-value ones that would make a bigger impact to her business and take her to her desired nine figures a year revenue target. Catherine was blown away by having this unconscious motivation brought to her conscious awareness.

Albert and Catherine's cases remind me of a story I heard on an NLP training course about an American businessman who met a humble fisherman while on holiday. The businessman, walking along the beach, notices a fisherman who seems to be taking life easily, and asks, 'What do you do around here?' The fisherman says, 'Oh, not much really. I catch a few fish during the day, sunbathe, then in the evening, I cook the fish and dine under the stars with my wife and kids.' The businessman looked bewildered, and asked, 'Why not catch more fish?'

'And then what?' asked the fisherman.

'Well, you could buy a bigger boat, and catch *even more* fish,' the businessman replied.

'And then what?' asked the fisherman.

'Then you could afford to have a fleet of ships and have dozens if not hundreds of fishermen catching fish for you!'

'And then what?'

'Then you could have a multinational fishing corporation that catches millions of fish, making you millions of dollars each year!'

'And then what?'

'Then, you could spend the rest of your days catching a few fish, sunbathing, and in the evening, you can dine under the stars with your wife and kids!'

This is, of course, a representation of how many of us think. We believe we first have to make more money or get to a certain level of status before we can have the thing we really want. As a child, I was always puzzled how many people dream of retiring somewhere hot and sunny. I remember asking one of my uncles, 'Why don't people just move there now?' And to this day, I felt I never had a satisfactory answer to this question. It's the reason why, at the age of twenty-nine, I left London and moved to sunny Gran Canaria. Why should I wait until I'm sixty or seventy?

Likewise, in your life, where have you been trying to achieve something by going from your starting point to goal A, thinking you will end up at goal B? In Albert's case, the goal was to earn £2 million (goal A), subconsciously thinking it would give him goal B (a happier marriage). But why go to the hassle of chasing goal A, when you can go straight for goal B, and avoid wasting time with goal A?

Starting point ⟶ Goal A ⟶ Goal B
Starting point ⟶ Goal B

Certainly, in my own life, one of my hidden motivations for wanting a girlfriend and to be wealthy and successful (goal A) has been to feel loved and worthy (goal B). But rather than chasing these extrinsic goals, I decided I could instead just do some work directly on goal B – raising my self-esteem. Having a girlfriend and being ultra-wealthy aren't totally in my control and are unstable foundations for self-esteem (what if my girl-friend leaves or I lose said wealth?). Whether I meet the love of my life, or FDBK becomes the next big thing in dating apps and ends up a 'start-up unicorn' (a business valued at $1 billion) isn't totally in my control, even if I'm very confident it will be successful. But what *is* in my control is how much inner work I do on my self-esteem.

In a nutshell

Most, if not *all*, of our actions have a deeper and hidden motiv-ation behind them – which typically boils down to nine different main motivations. As a result, our primary motivations can make us more susceptible to certain triggers and vices, such as anger, pride, deceit, envy, stinginess, fear, gluttony, lust and self-forgetting. But by asking yourself the questions shared in this chapter, you can raise your self-awareness and break free from such vices. Our hidden motivations can also affect our relation-ships and interactions with people, and lock us into unhealthy relational patterns, such as Love Avoidance, Love Addiction and Co-dependency.

The truth of our deeper motivations can sometimes be enlightening as well as disturbing, and it requires much courage to admit to ourselves the real reason why we are doing some-thing. But the truth can also set you free. If you can become more aware of your actions – and the deeper motivation as to *why* you are really doing them, you will stop sleepwalking through life; you will make the unconscious conscious and be freer to determine your own fate.

The main takeaway is this: have a think, and ask yourself, 'What's my *hidden* motivation?' You may have ulterior motives!

CHAPTER 5

What's Most Important to Me?

'When your values are clear to you, making decisions becomes easier.'

—ROY DISNEY

If you're anything like me, then you'll know the pain of having to make decisions. I often find decisions painful because I can get into analysis paralysis. For example, I have been known to spend up to three hours (if not longer) in shops trying to decide between two pairs of shoes! You too have perhaps been presented with similar, if not larger, dilemmas, such as do you file for divorce, leave your job, or, the most agonising of all, which font to choose for a presentation or a website.

As one of my mentors would remind me when I was a CEO: 'Being CEO means choosing between a *terrible* choice and a *catastrophic* choice.' What he meant was that there was no such thing as a perfect decision in business, only a good enough one, often with disadvantages either way you decide. Likewise, life in general is a series of choices: what you wear, what you eat, where you live, where you work and what you will do next. It's sometimes a bit overwhelming. Most of us want to live well. But how do we do it? How do we make positive choices for ourselves? The good news is that the self-coaching question, 'What's most important to me?', can rapidly resolve such dilemmas, as it forces you to look within and to prioritise your requirements.

Discovering your core values and priorities

When clients come to me for help with getting clarity around career direction and their life purpose, I usually start off by getting them to look at their core values and priorities. I first ask, 'What's most important to you?', and then we begin their self-discovery process. They might say things like love, family, joy, health, helping others, creativity and self-expression. I then have them turn their values into *priorities*. Often, we can get unhappy in life because we are not living in accordance with our deepest values and our highest priorities. I then have my client brainstorm some job roles and career paths that meet their priorities, and then get them to score their options out of ten as to how well each priority is met. This then gives my client a much clearer idea of how well each role can support who they truly are. If a role meets their higher priorities better, then that role is a better fit for them. This exercise can also be applied to decisions beyond career choices.

Finding your life purpose

Ikigai is a Japanese word that means 'reason for being' and it covers four fundamental areas which can be covered with four simple questions: *What am I good at?*; *What do I love?*; *What does the world need?*; and *What can I be paid for?* However, I'm going to offer a slight modification of Ikigai with one additional question:

1. What am I good at?

This can cover specific skills, such as computer programming, running or singing as well as more generic skills, such as being creative or thinking on your feet. Keep in mind your specific skills most likely have transferrable skills that come with them. For example, to be good at computer programming, you typically have to be good at problem-solving and understanding deeply technical concepts.

2. What do I love?

For example, this could be helping others, problem-solving, learning new things, travelling, making things, psychology, science, art, or home-making. And yes, it could even be chocolate.

3. What's most important to me?

Asking what the world needs is quite a big question, and one that my clients can struggle with. So instead I ask: *What's most important to you?* This helps to extract their core values. Perhaps it's aesthetics, tolerance, compassion, creative freedom, authenticity, community, conservation, justice – the list goes on. It could also be that having autonomy (being your own boss) might be more important to you. Certainly, for me, I generally don't like having a boss! Once you have discovered your core values, put them into order and turn them into *core priorities*. Then ask yourself *why* these are most important to you.

4. What can I be paid for?

This is where some of my clients can draw a blank also – and may require a bit of creative thinking. I certainly didn't realise that life coaching could be a genuine career that I could be paid very well for! You would be surprised what actual jobs there are out there these days. For example, you can genuinely be paid to:

- Play video games (eSports athlete, video games tester)
- Eat food (restaurant critic, taste master, flavourologist)
- Build Lego sets (Lego master builder)
- Make people laugh (comedian, author)
- Shop (personal shopper, mystery shopper)
- Use social media (influencer, social media manager)

Thus, you need to get past the outdated idea of a 'real job' in an office or a factory, as there's many more jobs and roles out there! Of course, some roles are more competitive than others, and may require some talent, dedication and perseverance. For example, one does not become a successful comedian overnight. It takes time to hone your craft and build up a reputation and a following.

5. **What's a common theme that's emerging?**
   After answering these questions, you hopefully might start to see a general theme emerging and can start to connect the dots.

If you find something that satisfies all of these areas, then congratulations, according to the Japanese principle of Ikigai, you have found your life purpose! However, my former supervisor and trainer Yannick Jacob, an existential coach with a masters in existential coaching, believes that we do not necessarily need to derive all of the aspects of Ikigai from our 'day job', but we can derive some from other areas of our life, such as volunteering, community, or side-gigs. This is certainly a valid way to approach Ikigai, though I would argue that forty to fifty hours spent on a job that you do not get satisfaction from is quite a waste of life, given how short and unpredictable life can be!

Often, many of us prioritise what we can be paid for, or perhaps what we are good at. But how many of us prioritise what we love, or what's most important to us? Paul Graham, co-founder of the world-famous YCombinator start-up accelerator, says that start-ups run on morale. Many careers do too. After four years of building it from the ground up, I decided to call it quits on giftgaming, which I only realised after taking a six-month break from it. After I came back, I discovered that I was out of *morale*. Heck, I didn't really care about life itself, let alone my own company. Looking back, I realise now that my need for meaning and purpose was completely unsatisfied. I was starting to feel so depressed as life just felt so pointless. It took courage for me to close down giftgaming: we had enough money in the bank to keep us going for another year, and before my mental breakdown, we were even on track to hitting P&L breakeven. But to quote Dr Michael Burry (of *The Big Short* fame): 'Making money is not like I thought it would be. It kills the part of life that is essential: the part that has nothing to do with business.'

I know that giftgaming's investors and supporters were very disappointed – some of whom were personal friends of mine. And it was a very tough call. However, I would have been doing a massive disservice to them by carrying on when I lacked the passion and enthusiasm that is required for a successful sale of the company. I was prioritising my mental health by shutting down giftgaming. Of course, since then, I have done much healing and growth work. I know myself much better. I have also addressed a lot of my childhood trauma, which crippled me the most.

After giftgaming, I realised that I really enjoy helping people, I'm good at it, the world needs it, and I can be paid for it. Unfortunately, a lot of entrepreneurship can lack one of the fundamental components of Ikigai: what the world *needs*. Not in terms of product-market necessarily (although sometimes in that sense too), but I mean in terms of what the world intrinsically needs; it doesn't necessarily *need* more advertising or more ad revenue, it needs more compassion, empathy and healing. It also needs more love, connection and less loneliness – which is one of the reasons why I co-founded FDBK. I want to help coach people on a massive scale to improve their dating profiles and thus increase their chances of success in finding that special someone or a new best friend.* There are *a lot* of lonely people in the UK. A study of over 55,000 people in 2018 found that 40 per cent of young people experience loneliness, and 16–24 and 35–44 year olds experience loneliness more often and more intensely than any other age groups.† This is certainly a national epidemic and a meaningful problem worth solving, especially as research has linked loneliness to poor physical and mental health (as explained in 'Social Needs', Chapter 2).

When I'm not writing, life coaching or doing entrepreneurial things, I do love playing the real-time strategy game, *Command & Conquer: Generals*. But does that mean I should be a pro-gamer? For me, that wouldn't work because it wouldn't feel fulfilling or meaningful enough. What about if you love sex – should

---

* I've made a few really good friends through dating! And even if you don't 'feel the spark', you can certainly be friends. I also met my best friend, Steve, at a singles party.
† BBC, 'Who feels lonely? The results of the world's largest loneliness study' – https://www.bbc.co.uk/programmes/articles/2yzhfv4DvqVp5nZyxBD8G23/ who-feels-lonely-the-results-of-the-world-s-largest-loneliness-study.

you become a porn star? Or, if you love being entrepreneurial and being your own boss – should you become a drug dealer? Probably not. Therefore, 'do what you love' isn't necessarily the best career advice. This is why you need to discover what's most important to *you*.

Play to your natural strengths

The best creature in nature is dependent on the task at hand. If it's building a dam? Beavers would win, no doubt. Catching flies in traps? Spiders. Blending in with the background? Chameleons. Being cute? Kittens, of course – no contest there. How about you? What are your intrinsic strengths and weaknesses? What do you think you might be best suited to naturally? For example, could this be leading, creating, innovating, problem-solving, and so forth?

A therapist once asked me, 'Why do birds sing?' I thought about it and replied, 'To mate or to signal danger, of course.' But then he asked, 'Why would they sing even if there's no danger, even if it's not mating season?' *Birds sing because it's what they are designed to do.* What if there were 8 billion unique types of human, each one with its own special gifts and quirks and dreams and thoughts. That's us. Believing that you are not special does help to reduce the ego, but at the same time can make us forget our own unique talents and strengths. You are a unique being; nobody else in the world is *you*. Not even your identical twin. Let that sink in for a moment.

GROWTH ACTION

Find your life purpose

Reflective questions

Answer the following questions to help you find more meaning and purpose in life:

1. What causes or issues do you feel really passionate about?
2. Who would really benefit from or need your help?
3. Who would you most like to serve – and why?
4. Where might your skills make a huge difference in society?
5. What's most important to you in life?
6. What legacy do you want to leave behind?
7. What similar challenges are others like you facing?
8. What has the 'tiny whisper of wisdom' been saying to you for some time but you've been too afraid to listen to?
9. If you had all the money in the world, how would you prefer to serve others – and why?
10. In forty years from now, what would you like to be known for – and why?

Prioritising your time

Where your treasure is, there your heart will be also

Fundamentally, what this saying means is: *where your time and money are invested will reflect where your priorities are.* I remember I once did a consultation with someone who said that they couldn't afford my coaching. I'm totally understanding of that; not many could afford to hire multi-Oscar-winning actress Meryl Streep for their next indie film, or world-renowned footballer Cristiano Ronaldo to play for their local football team. However, this prospective client also told me how they were travelling to the United States and had just bought an aerial drone with a camera so they could shoot some 'cool footage' for fun. *Good for them*, I thought. But I wondered where their priorities were. Clearly, they chose to prioritise travel and having fun over personal transformation, development and growth. Now, there's nothing wrong with that, but, in this case, it's not that they couldn't afford it, but rather, they chose not to prioritise it. There's a reason football teams invest tens of millions of pounds each year into players like Ronaldo; because they are serious about winning, and they want the very best of the best. Wherever your time, money and energy go, that's where your priorities lie.

Ask yourself, 'What's most important to me?' and have a look at whether your actions align with this. It could hold the key to why you feel unfulfilled, disconnected or discontented.

GROWTH ACTION

Assess where your precious time is going

1. Write down, in order, what is most important to you, e.g. health, family, fun, etc.
2. Work out how many hours a week you spend on:

   a. Sleep
   b. Work
   c. Exercise
   d. Relationships
   e. Leisure time
   f. Your dreams and goals
   g. Anything else that's important to you

3. As a percentage, how is your time being divided weekly for each area? To calculate this, do for each area:

   [number of weekly hours] ÷ 168 × 100

4. After having done this exercise, what could you change or do differently to increase your time allocation percentage to the things that matter most to you?

Checking your priorities are healthy

When I was younger, my priorities were, in this order:

1. Work
2. Money
3. Work (again)

4. Gym
5. Socialising
6. Sleep

However, I learned that this is not a healthy lifestyle at all. My mum used to warn me, 'You burn the candle at both ends, Nick.' In my youthful arrogance, I thought, *Yeah, yeah, yeah . . . it's not a big deal. I'll sleep when I'm dead!* That is, of course, until I found myself exhausted, burned out and getting sick a lot. When we are well, we have a thousand wishes, but when we are sick, we have only one. I now prioritise sleep, rest and health.

Why are they so important to you?

If I look back, work was so important to me because of what it represented. Firstly, I equated work with financial security. As a broke entrepreneur, getting the next round of funding was the difference between being able to pay the rent and eating three wholesome meals a day, and having to crash on a friend's sofa and eat baked beans. Secondly, being successful and possibly wealthy with my company would mean I would *be someone.* I wouldn't be just that programmer in a basement, or that unpopular kid that nobody wanted to go out with. I conflated work with self-esteem and belonging. Thirdly, I didn't want to let anyone down – especially my mentors and investors. For a while, I felt that I 'didn't deserve' to take weekends off as I felt that I needed to 'prove myself'.

Selfish v. service mode

Prioritising ourselves or others

If we only live for ourselves, when the storm of suffering comes, we will quickly collapse like a proverbial house built on sand. But if we live for a bigger purpose, one beyond ourselves, then your house will stand strong on a foundation of rock, even against the wildest storms. A saying we have in 12-Step Recovery is 'service is freedom from the bondage of self'. This is such a simple yet profound saying, meaning that we can experience relief from our own problems by serving others and setting our attention outwards, away from ourselves. If you think about who most of your fears and resentments revolve around, the answer is probably one person: *yourself.* Too often in our individualistic culture we are encouraged to focus on the *self;* self-esteem, self-development, self-empowerment, self-love, self-actualisation, self-fulfilment. Self, self, self. Paradoxically, in order to be our best selves, we must stop thinking only of ourselves. In order to break out of depression, we must stop being so introspective and start looking outwards. Our psyche needs input from sources beyond ourselves, for the brain is a *social* organ; it thrives on interaction and connection with others.

When I wrote this book, I was moving to a new flat. During this process, I realised the temporality of both my possessions as well as my very own existence on Earth. In a few days from now, a crack team of professional cleaners will come and erase any trace of my existence.

The next tenants of this property will probably not know or care who I was. And I do not know the tenants who lived here before me either. Yet, like those previous tenants, I have treated this flat as a permanent home. Likewise, do we not do the same with Earth and this life? Treating it as if it is where we will be for ever – when we won't. We're simply tourists passing through this particular space and time.

There are two types of tourist you typically encounter when you travel. The first is the considerate kind; they clean up after themselves, they don't mess with nature or historical artefacts, and generally they try to keep things nice for the next visitor. They respect the local laws and customs, as well as the locals themselves. Along the way as they pass other tourists, they might offer practical assistance, guidance or some hidden gems of wisdom they picked up from the locals and their own experience.

And then there's the loud and inconsiderate kind; they leave an absolute mess for the next visitor. They disrespect the locals and cause a nuisance for them. And even when they see other tourists in pain or struggling, rather than stop and ask if they can help them, they just carry on walking or perhaps pretend that they didn't see them. Perhaps they might come across an injured traveller but decide to just simply walk on by. This kind of tourist probably ends up either locked up abroad or banned for life from flying on various airlines.

We all like to think of ourselves as the considerate tourist, yet we've all been guilty of thinking of only ourselves, and even if we see someone struggling, we too often think 'someone else will help'. Haven't all of us, at some point in our life (some more than others), been guilty of being the second kind of traveller?

Service makes you less self-centred

Petty Officer Marcus Luttrell was a United States Navy SEAL who was part of Operation Redwings with SEAL Team 10 to carry out reconnaissance on a group of structures that were being used by Taliban militia and their leader. However, just hours after entering the target the area by helicopter, Luttrell and his squad were ambushed and came under heavy fire. Outgunned and outnumbered, the team had to fall back. In his book, *Lone Survivor*, Luttrell shares a personal account of events of what happened during Operation Redwings. Wounded and pinned down, the squad were in serious trouble, all of them having been shot multiple times, and starting to run low on ammunition.

Luttrell's squad leader, Lieutenant Michael Patrick Murphy, tried to call HQ several times for backup, but the mountainous terrain of Afghanistan's Kunar Province made communication impossible. Thus, Lt Murphy made a brave and selfless decision: he broke from cover to fight and climb his way to the top of a cliff so that he could get reception on his satellite phone to alert HQ that his squad were in immediate need of support. But doing so meant he had to directly expose himself to enemy fire.

Once he managed to sound the alarm with HQ, he then proceeded to engage the enemy until he was mortally wounded. Lt Murphy sacrificed his life for his comrades so that they could be helped. There is no greater love than this: that a person would lay down their life for the sake of their friends. All of us can take a leaf from Lt Murphy's book and instead of choosing to live only for ourselves, we can instead choose to give our lives to a greater cause. In fact, one motto of the US Navy is '*Non sibi sed patriae*', which translated from Latin means 'Not for self, but for country'. Perhaps we can slightly modify this slogan to '*Non sibi sed aliis*', or, loosely translated, 'Not for self, but for others'. Without service to a calling, purpose or mission greater than ourselves, we are doomed to meaningless, purposeless existential despair, and then, eventually, depression.

Too much focus on yourself can make you depressed

A young student who had experienced much suffering wanted to learn the secret of being happy from a wise old teacher. So, the teacher handed him a glass of water and put a cup of salt in it. Then he told the student to take a sip and asked, 'How does the water taste?', to which the student replied, 'Bitter.' The wise old teacher then took the student on a walk to a large freshwater lake and poured a cup of salt into it. Again, he asked the student to take a sip. So, the student bent down, leaned over and had a sip from the lake. Then the teacher asked, 'How does the water taste?', and the student replied, 'Fresh'. The teacher then asked, 'Can you taste the salt?' and the student replied, 'No.' The teacher smiled and said, 'The salt represents our pain in life. The amount of pain we have is the same. But the bitterness we taste depends on the container we put it in, whether you drink out of a cup or a lake. If you want to experience less pain, you must enlarge your view of life and become like this lake.'

Why am I single? Why doesn't anyone love me? Why must I sleep alone at night? When this way of thinking sets in, I find it really helpful to stop and ask myself, '*Who* or *what* am I serving?' If the answer is only myself, and it sometimes is, then I become *more* self-centred and *more* focused on my problems. As mentioned earlier, depression is an unhelpful, trance-like state of meaninglessness and hopelessness, often induced by severe stress or anxiety. Thus, this question also helps to bring more meaning to my suffering and my life, through connecting myself to a mission and a cause greater than myself.

In fact, one of the co-founders of the human givens psychotherapy school, Ivan Tyrrell, says that depressed people can be very *self-centred* in that the focus of their attention is often locked in on *themselves* and their problems and they have become too introspective. Thus, part of lifting depression is getting the client focusing *outwards*, such as through exercise, socialising, and being of service to others in their community – to get one out of one's own head. This approach is of course in stark contrast to traditional psychoanalytic therapy which involves *even more* introspection and focusing on past trauma, which, as Ivan says, is harmful and inadvisable for depression!

So, every time I feel sad, lonely, or fearful, I try to ask myself, 'What's my mission again? Who am I here to serve?' This then prompts me to do some soul-searching and reflecting. *Oh yes, that was the mission!* I then try to find a way to make myself useful and realign to my personal mission. And then a lot of my problems suddenly feel less relevant. When I'm truly in service, I forget all about my own suffering, almost like a legal high. As such, I've been single a few years and it actually feels good. I'm not the same desperate young man I once was; I am more than happy to wait for the right woman. And if I die alone? Well, at least I have fulfilled my purpose, lived a meaningful life and have served others. Ironically, not being so desperate and engaged with life probably makes one *more* attractive versus if one was to just wallow in sadness and self-pity!

As it happens, studies show that religious people are happier on average.* I suspect part of that reason is because many of them feel they are on a higher mission, one that transcends the pains of this life and this world, which gives them meaning and purpose, even in the face of suffering. They also tend to have much better community support. Studies have also shown them to be more 'civically engaged': they are more involved in community action. This no doubt requires a level of selflessness. During the coronavirus pandemic, one local church in Notting Hill was handing out free meals every day to the homeless. While many of us were cooped up, safe in our homes, local minister Chris Thackery of Westbourne Grove Church in Notting Hill and his loyal team of helpers were voluntarily feeding the homeless on the frontlines. Every. Single. Day. I happened to meet Chris serendipitously one day after having a panic attack. He is a wonderful humble man with a gentle and caring spirit.

---

* Pew Research Center, 'Religion's Relationship to Happiness, Civic Engagement and Health Around the World', 2019. https://www.pewforum.org/2019/01/31/religions-relationship-to-happiness-civic-engagement-and-health-around-the-world/ – accessed 25 October 2020.

He and his ministry regularly help the homeless, not just with food, but with practical things like the bureaucratic process of applying for housing and benefits, and warm showers.

We may have given homeless people spare change, or maybe the odd sandwich, but how many of us can say we have gone that extra mile to help them with benefits applications and emergency accommodation? Not many. But Chris certainly has and is a man I look up to in that regard.*

I suspect religious or spiritual people's happiness comes from them having a lesser degree of self-centredness and the focus on something *bigger* than themselves, as well as getting their need for community met. Note that ancient teachings have been telling us to serve others with wisdom such as 'love thy neighbour' and 'give and ye shall receive' for *thousands* of years, but it was only in 2011 that Dr Jennifer Crocker's psychology study (which we touched upon at the end of Chapter 1) found that selfless acts of service can in fact boost self-esteem and reduce symptoms of depression. Yet, many of us in the West can have the audacity to claim that modern psychology is on a par with enlightenment!

If you live only for yourself, one of two things will happen: one is that when the storm of suffering comes, and it's a case of not *if*, but *when*, then unless you have a mission that transcends the ego, you will become miserable. You may think, *Well, life is just suffering, why should I continue if I can't be comfortable and happy?* This is a very self-centred way of being. As a result, it will lead to depression. Why go on living if you feel you have nothing to live for? This is why happiness as a life objective in itself is problematic: because it cannot be sustained. In fact, I often joke to my clients: 'If you want to be happy all the time, then take drugs.' Because normal human life is not happy all the time. There will

---

* Being the selfless and humble man he is, I suspect Chris will thank me for saying this, and then point me to where he gets his generous spirit from and tell me to worship that instead of him!

be feelings of disappointment, sadness, anger, fear, shame, guilt, loneliness, there will be suffering, sickness and death of our loved ones, and the issue comes when we avoid feeling those things by taking a substance or indulging in a process.

The other outcome of living only for yourself is that once you achieve all you want to achieve, experience all there is to experience, and have all you want to have, what is there left to do? You don't need more money, more fame, more prestige; you have achieved much already. What is life now but a meaningless and hedonistic treadmill? This is why I believe some ultra-successful celebrities and homeless people can have one thing in common: a drug addiction. They can lack sufficient meaning and purpose, so what is there to do except get high to escape existential despair? Therefore, a mission or purpose greater than yourself is essential for psychological well-being, lest you succumb to meaninglessness and then clinical depression.

As well as thinking of serving others, you do of course need to keep in mind that your own life (in this world at least) is finite and limited.

Dying regrets

Death is a powerful motivator

'When a man knows he is to be hanged, it concentrates his mind wonderfully,' the eighteenth-century writer Samuel Johnson wrote. Death can be a very powerful motivator and can force us to refocus our priorities. Imagine that you were told you had only a few years left to live – what would you do? What would you prioritise? What would you de-prioritise?

A powerful exercise I do with my coachees is I ask them how old they are today. I then take that number and subtract it from eighty (the approximate average life expectancy in the UK as of 2020)* then multiply it by 365 (number of days in a year). Then I explain to them, 'This is the number of days you have left to live – in the *best-case* scenario.' There is no guarantee you will live to eighty years old, and this is assuming that you don't get cancer, have a heart attack, die in a car crash or choke on a pretzel. For example, if you are aged thirty reading this, then the number of days you have left to live would be:

$$(80 - 30) \times 365$$
$$= \textbf{18,250 days}$$

My clients are often floored when they find this out. It's like they have been told that they have a terminal illness. I have brought their mortality to the forefront, which then gets them to wake up and pay attention and it helps them realise that they need to start living and make that change *today*. It can certainly be a great way to help them push past any fears! To hammer home the point, I also remind them that with each day, that number goes down, and in just three years, it will have reduced by over 1,000! Now, this can seem like a bit of a rude awakening, but sometimes that is exactly what is needed to jolt someone into action. Sometimes the hardest prisons to leave are the most comfortable ones, so consider this exercise my metaphorical and existential cattle prod.

You are already terminally ill

Life has a 100 per cent mortality rate – so you are *already* terminally ill; you do not need to wait for a diagnosis. Therefore, I sometimes ask myself the question, 'If today were my last day

---

* Public Health England, 'Life expectancy in England in 2020', https:// publichealthmatters.blog.gov.uk/2021/03/31/life-expectancy-in-england-in-2020/ – accessed 14 April 2021.

on Earth, what would I regret *not* doing?' It's often the things we *haven't* done that we regret. Bronnie Ware, a palliative care nurse, worked with dying patients in their last days and recorded the most common dying regrets, which were:

1. 'I wish I'd had the courage to live a life true to myself, not the life others expected of me.'
2. 'I wish I hadn't worked so hard.'
3. 'I wish I'd had the courage to express my feelings.'
4. 'I wish I had stayed in touch with my friends.'
5. 'I wish that I had let myself be happier.'

If you were to die tomorrow (or even today!), which of these would you be most likely to regret? How often do you pull late nights at the office, at the expense of family time, leisure time, or time for pursuing your dreams and goals? As I've often told my clients, 'If you were hospitalised tomorrow, it would most likely be your family and friends that would show up – not your boss, your clients or your customers.'

One of my ex-girlfriends' fathers worked hard all of his life. After being a firefighter for many years, he then successfully set up a coaching company and worked very hard to work with some large businesses, executives and directors. Unfortunately, he contracted cancer in his sixties and died. Some of his dying words, which he passed on to my ex-girlfriend, were: 'On paper, I might be a millionaire. But what good is it now?' He worked hard his whole life, and just as he approached retirement age, he wasn't able to enjoy the spoils. We can spend our whole life prioritising money, security, 'winning the bread', or chasing prestige, title and status, that we can lose sight of what's most important and enduring. In the process of trying to improve our lives, we can forget to stop and smell the roses, to appreciate what we have in the present moment. You can always make more money, but you can *never* make more time.

To quote clergy member A. J. Reb Materi: 'So many people spend their health gaining wealth, and then have to spend their wealth regaining their health.' I have certainly been guilty of this myself at times. Thus, I occasionally coach myself by asking: 'Is money *really* more important than my health?' The answer is, of course, a resounding 'no'!

The time for change is today – not tomorrow

Occasionally, when I do consultations with prospective clients, they tell me they're 'not quite ready'. So, when *will* they be ready? When the moon perfectly aligns with Jupiter? When a cure for cancer is found? From my experience, those who don't strike while the iron is hot, don't end up working with me. This is likely because people get busy with work, with other commitments and priorities. I have done enough consultations to know this. Just because you are motivated to do something today, it doesn't guarantee you will be tomorrow, or next week. Similarly, just because an opportunity is available today, it doesn't mean it will be in a few weeks' or months' time.

As a young man, one of my biggest pet peeves is when older folk tell me, 'Oh you're still young, you've got plenty of time!' I imagine a lot of young people once thought this way too. And then before they know it, they're forty years old and in a job that they don't like, wondering whatever happened. The reality is that none of us knows when our last day on Earth will be. It could be ten years in the future, or, Heaven forbid, even tomorrow. Therefore, no one has the right to tell you that you've got plenty of time. You may not. I say this not to alarm you, but rather, to wake you up and motivate you to make those changes today – and not in the elusive tomorrow, which may not exist. So whatever dreams you want to realise, whatever you want to change, whoever you need to make amends to or tell them that you love them, start doing so *today*.

Of course, I'm not suggesting for a minute that you should – as one of my clients genuinely wanted – try to complete a PhD, run a dance troop, reform mental health in the UK, write a book, become a leading life coach and be a professional photographer all at once.

There's following your dreams, and then there's living in dreamland. This sounds like a recipe for burnout or fatigue, and, of course, said client was an Enneagram Type 7 (The Visionary), who wished to 'experience it all'. I explained to them that they could do anything, but not *everything*, not at the same time at least. What I'm asking you to do instead is to prioritise. There are only twenty-four hours in the day, and you need to sleep anywhere from seven to twelve of them. You have less time than you think. You also need to make time for rest, relaxation, recreation and relationships, or else you will go insane. A good rule of thumb to remember is whenever you say 'yes', you are saying 'no' to something else. This is another good reason why you need to ask, 'What's most important to me?'

Balance is key

The awareness of our mortality needs to be balanced out with some faith in the future. If we act as if we are going to live for ever, and that things will always be the same, this may make us complacent as well as procrastinate. However, if we didn't have any faith in the future at all, and live as if we would die tomorrow, then we would not give any thought to planning for the future.

Marrying anyone because you're scared of dying alone is a bad idea; being desperate for a relationship is a recipe for ending up in the *wrong* one. In fact, one of my previous clients, Tina, an accountant in her early forties, wouldn't leave her partner despite the fact he was very abusive to her. This was because she *believed* she was too old and running out of time. 'This could be my last shot at love!' she exclaimed. Of course, this was most likely a form of catastrophic thinking – that unless Tina stayed in her toxic relationship, she would be doomed to die alone! Like the rest of us, Tina does not have a crystal ball, nor can we predict the future with great accuracy.

It's possible to keep awareness of your mortality *and* have faith that the future is full of opportunities for you to seize.

GROWTH ACTION

Reflect on your mortality

1. Do the following calculation:

    (80–your age) × 365

    This is how many days you have left to live in the *best*-case scenario. How many days do you have?

2. If you were to die tomorrow:

    i)   What dying regrets would you have?
    ii) What will you start changing today to ensure you don't end up with those regrets?

3. If you had only four years left to live, how might your priorities change – and what would you do differently?

In a nutshell

When you know what's most important to you, it becomes much easier to make decisions, whether they are small ones, such as deciding whether you should have a slice of cake or a salad, or bigger ones, such as whether you should pack up your bags and leave the UK for sunnier climes. Knowing what's most important can also be used to help you find your dream career or life purpose, as well as filter out life choices that don't align with your values and priorities. Of course, you do need to check if your priorities are healthy and not overly self-centred. Many of us can prioritise ourselves over serving others at times, and this can be a recipe for depression, as we can become too introspective and then dwell too much on our own problems. We must therefore look to a mission and purpose greater than ourselves, one that transcends our ego.

Being reminded of our own mortality and our limited time on Earth can force us to re-evaluate our priorities. Of course, we have to balance out our existential fear of death with some faith and hope in that tomorrow will be brighter, or else we will fall into despair and depression as *hope for the future* is a fundamental human need (as I explained in Chapter 2). In the next chapter, we will explore how our beliefs can affect this crucial need, as well as our self-esteem.

CHAPTER 6

Are My Beliefs Serving Me?

'He who has a why can bear almost any how.'

—FREDRICH NIETZSCHE

A woman is swimming out at sea. She begins to get tired and realises she is in trouble and risks drowning. A group of people on a nearby boat are shouting something at the woman, but she cannot hear; she is too preoccupied carrying a large backpack with her, which weighs her down like a heavy rock. The woman realises that the people on the boat are shouting, 'Drop the bag!' But she yells back, 'No, it's my bag!' Unwilling to let go of the backpack, the woman gets more tired and the backpack causes her to get dragged down beneath the surface of the water. She tries kicking her legs frantically, and manages to get a brief breath of air, and again she hears the people on the boat yell, 'Drop the bag!' The woman is stubborn though. She doesn't want to let go of the backpack. It contains various things she has collected over the years, which she considers precious. Finally, after the woman can no longer keep herself afloat, as she sinks deeper into the water and is about to drown, she reluctantly lets go of her bag. The moment she does, she rapidly floats up to the surface and takes in the sweetest breath of air ever in her life. She ends up feeling hugely relieved, and for the first time in her life, she realises just how much that backpack had weighed her down and made her sink deeper into despair.

The story you just read is a variation of a story I have heard in addiction recovery circles, known as 'Drop the Rock'. In addiction recovery, people's lives literally depend on their ability to change. However, it often takes people hitting rock bottom for them to become willing to change. Many of those in recovery may do so reluctantly and may resist suggestions to change until the pain of remaining the same becomes greater than the pain of change. Of course, it does not need to be this way with you! You simply have to be willing to believe something new and not be too attached to your old beliefs and ways of thinking.

If you are totally content with your life, then there is no reason to change your beliefs. However, if you are unhappy with yourself or your life, then *something* has to change within you. If nothing changes, then *nothing* changes.

You may not be willing to let go of your old beliefs just yet. Yet, although it is painful for the ego, by letting go of what no longer serves us, we become more wholesome beings.

Challenge your psychological beliefs

You become what you believe

Imagine for a moment that overnight, you lost all your memory, and when you woke up, you forgot who you were. Suppose that upon waking up, you're told you who you are. How would you carry yourself and behave if you were told that you were one of the following:

- A respected tech billionaire
- A member of the elite SAS military regiment and they wanted you back
- A front-cover model of a fitness magazine and you'd recently been named most attractive person in the world

Now compare this with if you were told you were:

- A homeless person addicted to crack with serious mental disorders
- A washed-up musician whose one-hit wonder nobody really remembers any more
- The 'star' of a viral internet video about how fat and ugly you are

How might these given identities affect how you think, feel and behave? In my own journey, I began to believe I was *already* a successful life coach when I was first starting out; I began to 'act as if'. What would a 'successful life coach' do exactly? They would do a lot of training, professional development, learn from the best, and would carry themselves with confidence. I believe this played a big part in making my coaching practice what it is today, and how I ended up coaching celebrities, clinical psychologists, psychiatrists and neuroscientists. Similarly, once I started to believe I was *already* attractive, I started making more decisions to reinforce that identity, such as eating healthily, exercising regularly, dressing well, working on my tan and getting my beauty sleep. Here, I used the good side of Labelling Theory, which I shared in Chapter 1. Thus, if you call yourself 'fat' or 'ugly', you may be more likely to do behaviours to reinforce those labels. So, start calling yourself 'sexy' and imagine what that would *feel* like. How would a 'sexy' or 'fit' person choose to behave? How would a 'fat' or 'ugly' person choose to behave? *You become what you believe you are.*

You achieve what you believe

In the 1950s, many people had tried – and failed – to run a mile in under four minutes. And thus, it became known as the 'four-minute barrier' – the fastest possible time to run a mile. That was until one day, in 1954, athlete Sir Roger Bannister ran it in 3:59.4. Just forty-six days later, an Australian runner, John Landy, broke the four-minute barrier again, with a time of 3:58. Since then, at the time of writing this, nearly 1,500 runners have gone on to break an 'impossible' barrier.

Certainly, in my own coaching practice, I have heard the following be deemed 'impossible':

- Letting go of a well-paid job to pursue a dream or calling (I have done this myself a couple of times!)
- Making it as an actress at age forty (Dame Judi Dench didn't get her 'big break' in film until she was 61, which was when she played M, James Bond's boss, in the blockbuster *Goldeneye*)
- Changing a career after twenty-plus years' experience at age fifty (Colonel Sanders started the international fast-food chain, KFC, at age 65)

Are there beliefs in your life where you think something is likewise impossible?

GROWTH ACTION

Identify limiting beliefs

Reflect on the following questions:

1. i) In terms of positive traits, what do you believe
    you are not currently?
    ii) Now imagine you *were* that trait – how
    would you behave differently? What different
    choices would you make?

2. i) What do you consider 'impossible' in terms of
    your dreams or aspirations?
    ii) How do you know *for sure* that they're
    impossible?

How to start challenging unhelpful beliefs

There are various techniques to challenge or change limiting
beliefs – and Cognitive Behavioural Coaching (CBC) is one of
them. It is built on the premise that our beliefs affect our emotions and actions. Typically, in CBC, there are five components
in the 'ABCDE Model':

- **Activating events** – which events have triggered a
  certain reaction?
- **Beliefs** – what do we believe about ourselves, others,
  the world, etc.?
- **Consequences** – how we feel and act in response to
  the event in the context of our beliefs.

- **Disputation** – disproving the old beliefs.
- **Effective new beliefs** – that can replace the old beliefs.

The premise of CBC is that it is not the events that determine our reactions, but, rather, our *beliefs* through which we experience the events; the *activating event* does not directly trigger *consequences*. Two people can experience the same event and have *very* different reactions based on their beliefs.

A coaching client of mine, Julie, was a talented architect in her mid-thirties. She was in a relationship and had a child, but then the relationship ended, so she focused on bringing up her child on her own for a while. However, over time she realised she was lonely. Unfortunately, she had some confidence issues around dating. A few bad experiences had stopped her from looking, and created the belief that she was never going to meet a partner as she had a child already.

So, I applied the ABCDE Model with her:

Activating events:

- Confident people approaching her in a bar
- When she enters a new environment
- When she's considering trying something sociable

Beliefs:

- 'I'm not going to meet a partner because I have a child already.'

Consequences:

- Feeling uncomfortable around people
- Putting off meeting new people and staying single

Another person could be approached in a bar and their reaction, as well as the outcome, could be very different if their belief instead was: 'I'm an attractive and desirable person.'

But instead, Julie believed she was undesirable, which caused her to isolate herself and stay single. I challenged Julie on her beliefs and asked her, 'Where are your beliefs *not* true?' Julie came up with the following:

Disputation:

- There was a man she liked who didn't mind she had a child
- One of her friends had dated women with kids
- Another man she liked already had a child of his own
- Her friend's stepfather took on two boys who weren't his own

Clearly, the belief that Julie wasn't going to meet a partner because she already had a child is a *generalisation* – a type of 'thinking trap'. The above are solid counter-examples of where her belief is not true.

We then explored what the new more effective and more accurate belief would be. Together, Julie and I created the following:

Effective new beliefs:

- While some men may prefer to date women without children, some men may not mind either way
- If a man does mind me having a daughter, he is not right for me

Initially, Julie was resistant to changing her beliefs; they had kept her safe from rejection for a long time. However, after applying the ABCDE Model, Julie began to see that her beliefs around men were not working for her and were simply not accurate.

Unhelpful belief patterns

Beliefs are often over-generalisations created from isolated incidents. In Julie's case, we saw how her beliefs were a type of unhelpful belief pattern – the trap of over-generalisation. Here are other traps you need to watch out for:

- **Black-and-white thinking** – Also known as 'all-or-nothing' thinking. Thinking in absolutes, for example, believing you are totally perfect or an absolute failure, with no room for shades of grey in between. To escape this trap, ask yourself, 'What middle ground might I be missing? What other interpretations could there be?'
- **Fortune-telling** – Making predictions about the future based on little or no evidence: 'I just *know* I'm going to fail.' The way to escape this trap is to ask yourself, 'How do I know *for sure* this event is going to happen?'
- **Catastrophising** – Assuming the absolute worst-case scenario and blowing events out of proportion. For example, 'I'm going to die alone because I haven't met a partner at the age of thirty'. To dismantle this trap, ask yourself, 'Are things *really* as bad as I think they are?'
- **Personalisation** – When you unnecessarily blame yourself. For example, if someone does not reply to a message or perhaps frowns at you, you assume it is because of *you*. For example, 'They obviously did this because of me.' To break out of this trap, ask yourself, 'What other reasons could there be for this happening

that do not involve me?' (Refer back to the habits of high self-esteem people at the end of Chapter 1.)

- **Emotional reasoning** – Believing something is true just because you feel it is true, without solid evidence. Ask yourself, 'What evidence is there to support this?'
- **'Should' and 'must'** – Making unrealistic demands on yourself or others by using statements such as 'I must ...' or 'I should ...' To break out of this trap, ask yourself, 'Why must things be done this way? What other ways could there be to do this?'

Some other traps to be aware of include:

- **Comparison** ('*Everyone else* my age is married with kids, so there must be something wrong with me!')
- **Genetic fallacy** ('I'll *always* be depressed / anxious because my mum had depression / anxiety.')
- **Fatalism** ('I'll *never* be/have [xyz].')
- **Utopianism** ('I'll be happy *when* I have / achieve lots of money / a partner / kids / ... ')
- **Self-labelling** ('I can't do [xyz] because I'm an introvert/extrovert/empath/ ... ')
- **Globalising** ('I failed at my job / my marriage / the competition. I fail at *everything*!' – remember from Chapter 1 about the behaviours of low and high self-esteem people.)

Reflecting on your own unhelpful beliefs, do they fall into any of these traps?

Your beliefs may be unrealistic or unhelpful

One belief that Julie had around finding her dream man (which was eroding her self-esteem) was that 'it should be easy'. The story she told herself was, 'If I was attractive, then surely it should be easy.' This belief was not helpful to her self-esteem. So, I asked what her requirements were. And she came back with this list:

- Earns a similar salary (£70,000 a year or higher – which was the top 6 per cent of earners in the country in 2019)
- Is very handsome (within top 10 per cent of most attractive men)
- Is intelligent (within top 20 per cent of most intelligent men)
- Lives locally (in the London area)
- Must be single (no married men looking for a mistress)
- Must be aged forty to forty-nine

So, I did some calculations with Julie: there were approximately 4.5 million males living in London in 2019, and the percentage of people in the UK who earn over £70,000 (before tax) is around 6 per cent (top 94th percentile). So that's approximately 270,000 men. Of those men, only 10 per cent were going to be attractive enough for Julie. So that left 27,000 men. As my client wanted only the most intelligent men in the top 20 per cent of intelligence, that then narrowed down the pool of bachelors to 5,400. Assuming that 50 per cent are married as per estimates from the Office of National Statistics in 2019, that narrowed it down to 2,700 men. As she wanted a man in his forties, that was approximately going to be 14 per cent of the 2,700, which left 378 potential men. In the whole of London. To find one of those 378 eligible bachelors out of the potential 4.5 million males is no easy feat! Furthermore, this didn't even account for chemistry and emotional availability. Even if she lowered her standards a bit, and went for the top 20 per cent of attractive men, that's still only 756 men out of millions. However, the good news is that there's certainly enough potential life partners that meet her requirements if it doesn't work out with one of them. Of course, all of this was just an estimate based on some sensible assumptions, and I'm sure a professional statistician would have done a better job calculating the precise number of eligible bachelors than me! In any case, the belief that 'it should be easy' was loosened, and Julie started to feel better about herself (note the switch from blaming herself to looking for explanations that don't involve her, as explained in Chapter 1).

Your beliefs may be out of date

I shared with Julie a useful NLP presupposition: 'the past does not equal the future'. Just because something has happened in the past, it does not mean it will happen again in the future – just ask any gambler! They may hit it big one week, but the next week they may lose it all. Similarly, in the UK it may be sunny one day (or one *hour*) and pouring down with rain the next. What may have been true in the past, may not be true now.

Often our beliefs are subconsciously created as a result of events that happened to us. For example, one belief I had was 'I don't belong.' I realised that many people created this story in the past. For example, my mother, who would speak Romanian to her friends and some relatives, never taught me Romanian, so I didn't understand what she was saying. Or male relatives, who used to shame me for not watching football and for preferring to play video games. And bullies at school (who loved football) were racist to me because of my Romanian heritage. That story may have been true back then – perhaps I didn't belong at the school I went to. But, most importantly, *is this belief true today?* The answer for me is, no, it is not. You may also notice the other thinking traps this belief falls into such as all-or-nothing thinking (I don't belong *at all*) as well as over-generalising (I don't belong *anywhere*).

Think about your life and your unhelpful beliefs – how did those beliefs come about? Are they still true today?

In CBC, a crucial further step after identifying your beliefs in the ABCDE Model (after *ABC*) is *D* and *E*: disputation of old beliefs and establishing effective new beliefs. I sometimes like to refer to these new beliefs as 'the more accurate beliefs'.

As an example, to counteract my belief that 'I don't belong', here is the evidence that this is not true:

- I belong to humanity and Earth because all humans do
- I belong to 12-Step addiction recovery groups and with my fellows in recovery as I have addictive behaviours that need managing to prevent relapse
- I have a handful of friends who I have common interests with

The limitations of cognitive approaches

It should be noted that some beliefs may need more than a cognitive (intellectual) approach, as they can be created from intense emotional experiences such as trauma and upsetting events. Like any tool, CBC has its uses as well as its limitations. Thus, the best coaches and therapists ought to be trained in a wide variety of different approaches and methods, as no one technique or approach is suitable for every person or problem.

Some beliefs may require us to not only *think* differently, but also, to *experience* and *feel* things differently. This can be the case where you know something intellectually, but you don't feel it – such as with phobias and strong emotional triggers. In which case, working with the unconscious mind, such as through hypnosis may be required (which I'll cover more in the next chapter).

Your beliefs may not be your own

One of my clients – David, a company director – complained that he was suffering from procrastination. The issue we had narrowed down in our coaching session was that he had a limiting belief: 'I can't compete.' Upon exploring this further, we realised he had another belief: 'the world is a hyper-competitive place'.

So, we delved deeper and I asked David what messages he got from his parents in his childhood, and he came up with the following:

- 'You must compete'
- 'You must make a lot of money'
- 'You must buy a house'
- 'You must get married'
- 'You must get into a top university'

He then told me what messages he got from school:

- 'You must get into a top university'
- 'You must get top marks'
- 'You must win at sports day'

Finally, we explored messages he got from his friends:

- 'You must be successful to be one of us'

This approach of looking at unconscious messages we received in the past is what psychology professionals would call 'psycho-dynamic' – an exploration into unconscious forces operating in the mind. In this line of questioning, I revealed how David's past had been unconsciously affecting his present. Based on all the messages he had received from various sources, it's no wonder that he believed that the world was a competitive place!

After taking David through this exercise, he began to realise that this belief was not his own and was created by others, which he then adopted. This was an important step to David seeing the fallacy of his own thinking and to breaking the belief that was no longer serving him. In this case, believing he lived in a competitive world made him feel that he could not compete.

Think about your own beliefs for a moment: are they *really* your own, or are they subconsciously created from childhood messages that others have given you about the world?

How childhood experiences can affect our spiritual beliefs

I was certainly surprised to learn after reading *The Road Less Travelled* by the American psychiatrist Dr M. Scott Peck, that our conceptions of what 'God'* is like can be heavily biased and influenced by our early childhood experiences. When we were children, if our parents were harsh and unforgiving, we are more likely to have a conception that if there is a 'God', then they are also this way. Our first experiences of an all-powerful deity came from our parents. We depended on them for survival, protection and provision; they were once omniscient and omnipotent giants, and we were their little seedlings. Similarly, the 'Father Wound' in psychology theory (popularised by Professor Emeritus of Psychology, Paul Vitz) is the idea that if you had an absent or abusive father, you could be more likely to think of 'God' being non-existent or a tyrant. Just as we can develop an unconscious negative bias against ourselves (as we saw with low self-esteem in Chapter 1), we can also develop an unconscious bias about existential matters too, because of our past conditioning and upbringing.

Psychological beliefs play a part in determining our

---

* I use the word 'God' in quotes to mean a non-religious God, and basically, an all-powerful all-knowing creator and deity.

self-esteem as well as impacting our mental health and happiness. Our *existential* beliefs – our beliefs around the meaning of life, death and the afterlife – do as well. In the next section, we're going to explore existential beliefs and models for making meaning from life.

GROWTH ACTION

Banish limiting self beliefs

Apply the ABCDE model to your beliefs.

1. Make a list of your most limiting and negative self-beliefs. For example, 'I'm not good enough.'
2. Next, write down who created these beliefs and how they came about. What messages did you receive growing up and who from? How did these beliefs come about?
3. Then, come up with as much evidence or counter-arguments as you can to challenge the beliefs. What do you learn about your old beliefs?
4. Now write down what belief would be the *counter-belief* or the *more effective belief*. What evidence is there to support this new belief?

The importance of existential beliefs

Is there any greater meaning to life?

This is the question that many philosophers and deep thinkers have tried to answer: *why are we here*? The answers range from, 'there really is no point at all and it's all meaningless', to where every thought and action matters and has consequences both now and in the afterlife. Now you may say, 'Well, life's a bit pointless anyway, isn't it?' and perhaps you might want to get back to binge-watching TV shows or scrolling endlessly through social media on your phone. But this attitude won't help you get through tough times – as I know from my own experience. So, we must address this question. It's not a case of if suffering comes, but *when*, which makes it imperative to think about the meaning of life now. One thing is for certain: you are going to experience some form of suffering in this life, if you haven't already.

How beliefs can no longer serve you

Before 12-Step Recovery, I was very anti-religious and anti-spiritual – I absolutely resented going to meetings. The programme I attended was built on spiritual foundations, similar to that of Alcoholics Anonymous (AA), but for people with work addiction. Eventually, I got involved in volunteering, in supporting others, whether it was just creating space, listening or providing feedback and mentoring others who needed emotional support. I enjoyed doing this, especially when people had told me I had really helped them. I later became the de facto secretary (the person who facilitates the meeting) for the 12-Step group I had first joined five years ago! And as I got more involved in 12-Step Recovery, slowly, the workaholic disease lessened its grip on me, as did my other addictions. I no longer drink six coffees a day. I get plenty of sleep. I take at least one full day a week off. I say no to a lot now – because I have more faith that there will be enough time, money and love. I also make time for others, for friends and for family, and, of course, for my own self-care. In the deepest throes of work addiction, I could skip meals and basic self-care such as showers and brushing my teeth. I now delegate less important tasks and try not to do everything myself – and this is largely down to the fact that my beliefs changed around my connection to the universe, to life itself, as well as around what money and success mean.

As a result of my beliefs changing, I became less selfish and more serene. And as I continue to practise the principles of 12-Step Recovery in my life, I find one day at a time, my anxiety further decreases, and my serenity increases. And this was because I became willing to let go of my old ideas and beliefs. But in order to do so, I had to first be brought to my knees. Sometimes, suffering can have way of humbling us human beings – and I *had* to be humbled in order to change.

What I learned from my journey is that we must fundamentally ask ourselves, with an honest and open heart and mind, 'Are my beliefs serving me?' In my case, they certainly were not. As I look back at my former militant atheist days, I realise the belief that I had of having to do it all myself, the idea of total self-will and self-reliance did not serve me at all; it just made me a total control freak and workaholic. Why should I stop working if I truly believe there is nobody or nothing out there to help me or provide for me? The toxic hustle culture of 'you make your own luck' and 'no days off!' certainly does not help anyone with workaholism.

Before I discovered 12-Step, I would say I was not only a believer in atheism, but also *nihilism*.

Nihilism ('Everything is meaningless')

Nihilism is a complex philosophical concept, but in a nutshell, is an existential view where nothing fundamentally means anything in this universe. Some can find this existential view of life liberating because it means that there's no need to get so stressed about anything, given that none of it really matters, and we're all doomed to oblivion anyway! However, there can be a darker side to sinking too deeply into nihilism, in that it can predispose one to existential despair and meaninglessness; if you believe life is pointless and it's all for nothing, you are more likely to get depressed. Nihilism can then become a recipe for addiction, given that meaning, purpose and hope for the future are fundamental human needs. As respected psychoanalyst and clinical social worker Dr Erica Komisar says, 'Nihilism is fertiliser for anxiety and depression.' Dr Komisar goes as far as to recommend in her professional opinion that even if you don't believe in God yourself, you should *lie* to your children that you do, because it's better for their psychological well-being for them to believe there is a God and Heaven. As she said in an interview with the *Wall Street Journal*:

> The idea that you simply die and turn to dust may work for some adults, but it doesn't help children. Belief in Heaven helps them grapple with this tremendous and incomprehensible loss. In an age of broken families, distracted parents, school violence and nightmarish global-warming predictions, imagination plays a big part in children's ability to cope.[*]

She may well be right. A study of approximately five thousand carried out by Harvard researchers examined how being raised in a family with religious or spiritual beliefs affects mental health.[†] Children or teens who reported attending a religious service at least once a week scored higher on psychological well-being measurements and had lower risks of mental illness. Weekly

---

[*] 'Don't Believe in God? Lie to Your Children', *Wall Street Journal* – https://www.wsj.com/articles/dont-believe-in-god-lie-to-your-children-11575591658 – accessed 1 February 2021.

[†] Ying Chen and Tyler J. VanderWeele, 'Associations of Religious Upbringing With Subsequent Health and Well-Being From Adolescence to Young Adulthood: An Outcome-Wide Analysis', *American Journal of Epidemiology*, 187:11 (November 2018), 2355–2364. https://doi.org/10.1093/aje/kwy142.

attendance was associated with higher rates of volunteering, a sense of mission, forgiveness, and lower probabilities of both drug use and early sexual initiation. Another study consisting of over a hundred thousand health care professionals in the US found that those who had attended religious services weekly had a 68 per cent lower hazard of 'death from despair' among women and a 33 per cent lower hazard among men compared with those who never attended.*

Of course, while these churchgoers' innate human needs for community and belonging are being met, many of them are also getting their existential needs met, such as meaning and purpose, as well as hope for the future. The need to be able to make sense of suffering in a meaningful way is especially vital when you are a health care professional who is seeing sickness, suffering and death on a regular basis. Evidently, nihilism is not optimal for mental health and well-being.

Finding meaning in life without religion

While religion certainly has its benefits, it is not without its own problems (such as dogma, corruption and extremism), given that religious organisations are run by flawed human beings, after all. There are, of course, other ways we can derive meaning in life without religion. The human givens approach highlights three important ways to find meaning in our lives:

- By being stretched and challenged. Perhaps it could be to complete a marathon (a *running* marathon, not a TV series!), write a book, get into shape – or any other kind of personal goal that stretches us.

---

* Y. Chen, H. K. Koh, I. Kawachi, M. Botticelli, T. J. VanderWeele, 'Religious Service Attendance and Deaths Related to Drugs, Alcohol, and Suicide Among US Health Care Professionals', *JAMA Psychiatry*, 77:7 (2020), 737–744. http://dx.doi.org/10.1001/jamapsychiatry.2020.0175.

- Having people or animals who need us. This could be through children (your own or those of friends and relatives), older relatives or partners we care for, or having pets.
- Serving others through a cause that is greater than yourself, such as a charity, an organisation, or a community.

Other ways we can also find more meaning and purpose include:

- Doing meaningful and fulfilling work: whether it's for your dream career, your own business, or work that just makes your heart sing (whether it's creating art, programming, writing, or home-making). How to find this soul-nourishing kind of work is covered in more depth back in Chapter 5 ('What's Most Important to Me?').
- Viewing suffering through existential beliefs, such as a test from the universe, or part of a bigger cosmic plan (such as the *Cosmic Tapestry* model which I'll talk about below).
- Turning personal suffering into a challenge or an obstacle to overcome and turning it into a story of personal triumph and resilience (such as with the *Hero's Journey*).

Using the Cosmic Tapestry to make sense of suffering

There was once a man who had a farm. One day he noticed a wild horse had wandered on to his field. He couldn't believe his luck: he'd got a free horse. He was happy with life. But the next day, the horse ran off, and the man became angry with life. However, the horse came back, bringing with it five other horses! The man was ecstatic and called his son over to celebrate. His son, however, tried to ride one of the horses, fell, and broke his leg, and ended up having to walk on crutches. The man was angry with life again. But the next day, the army came into the village and was forcibly conscripting all the able-bodied young men. When they saw the state of the man's son, they passed him over. As a result, the man's son avoided being killed on the battlefield and got to live a long life. His son was even able to care for him as the man entered old age and couldn't run the farm any more. Thus, the man was happy with life again.

One model I propose for making sense of suffering is the *Cosmic Tapestry* model. The idea of this model is that multiple negative events may at first appear arbitrary, but, in fact, are connected and eventually lead to a structured plan of a greater good. A tapestry up close and behind the scenes is often messy, complicated and makes no sense at all; it looks like organised chaos at best. But as we move further away, the most beautiful picture starts to emerge, and the messiness makes sense. Likewise, in life, there may be things you have experienced which were horrendous at the time, but further into the future, may have led to some good. I for one wouldn't have chosen to become a life coach had I not been through all of the trauma in my childhood (and I probably wouldn't have had the opportunity to become a published author either!). Several psychotherapists I know also wouldn't be doing their profession had they not gone through what they had in their own personal lives (the 'wounded healer'* comes to mind). The coronavirus pandemic, despite millions of deaths and huge economic losses, has led to some positive changes. For example, less global pollution thanks to fewer cars on the road and

---

* A 'wounded healer' is someone who works in the helping profession because they have been wounded themselves and knows how it feels.

aeroplanes in the sky, as well as safer sex in society (meaning less unwanted children and STIs).* One study of over 1,500 people even found that the coronavirus pandemic resulted in positive outcomes for them, such as being able to rest, work from home more and even feel more socially connected.† Clearly, there are silver linings to some clouds.

Of course, not all suffering can seem immediately meaningful, and we should hear and comfort those who are in pain, rather than offer unhelpful platitudes such as 'everything happens for a reason'. Suffering can be very painful, and the best we can do at times is to weep with those who weep and mourn with those who mourn. But as finite and limited human beings, we cannot possibly know or understand how an event today might lead to a greater good in the future. There's no denying that longer-term good can come from negative events, and the Cosmic Tapestry model is one that can help us to make sense of suffering. To quote Steve Jobs: 'You can't connect the dots looking forward; you can only connect them looking backwards. So, you have to trust that the dots will somehow connect in your future. You have to trust in something – your gut, destiny, life, karma, whatever.'

If you have a meaningful explanation for suffering, you will be one of the happiest people in the world – because there is much suffering to be had or seen in this broken world, and being able to make sense of suffering, no matter how bad it gets, will keep you going and give you a sense of meaning and purpose that overrides the pain. If, however, your explanation for suffering is lacking, or you believe all suffering is simply bad luck, and there's no greater meaning, then you are at risk of not getting your intrinsic need

---

* B. Nelson, 'The positive effects of Covid-19', *BMJ*, 369 (May 2020), m1785. doi:10.1136/bmj.m1785 – https://www.bmj.com/content/369/bmj.m1785.
† M. Gijzen, *et al.*, 'The Bittersweet Effects of Covid-19 on Mental Health: Results of an Online Survey among a Sample of the Dutch Population Five Weeks after Relaxation of Lockdown Restrictions', *International Journal of Environmental Research and Public Health*, 17:23 (4 December 2020), 073. doi: 10.3390/ijerph17239073 – https://pubmed.ncbi.nlm.nih.gov/33291765/.

for meaning and purpose met. As explained in Chapter 2, unmet existential needs can make us mentally unwell, and depressed people often exhibit a sense of meaninglessness.

GROWTH ACTION

Apply the Cosmic Tapestry model to your life

1. Write down a list of major or meaningful positive events in your life.
2. For each event, write down a list of negative events that eventually led up to the positive event.
3. What have you learned from doing this exercise?

Turning suffering into challenges with the Hero's Journey

The *Hero's Journey* is a popular storytelling model created by Joseph Campbell. Although it's usually applied to fiction, you can also use the model to see your problems as challenges to be overcome and learned from. You can learn to thrive in spite of your battles. The Hero's Journey can help you to reframe your problems as *challenges* to be overcome, much like how the hero of a story must overcome trials and tribulations, and after doing so, they acquire some sort of new-found character development or gift (the stage of 'transformation' in the Hero's Journey model) and return home a true hero. Fantasy novels and films such as *Lord of the Rings* and the *Harry Potter* series usually follow this model. Stories and legends have been around for thousands of years – and ever since we used to gather around fires, stories have been used to teach, inspire and heal. When we hear a story, our brain can unconsciously look for similarities to how the character relates to us and, in turn, give us hope, wisdom and motivation for our own challenges and lives. When I was building FDBK, I found it entertaining and motivating to watch the comedy TV series *Silicon Valley*, as the protagonist, Richard Hendrix and his company, Pied Piper, have to overcome many, many entrepreneurial challenges – some of which I can certainly relate to!

A lot of very successful people have had to overcome some kind of challenge, both in fictional stories, as well as real life. Abraham Lincoln, for example, failed in business, survived a nervous breakdown, suffered the death of his fiancée and was defeated in *three* elections. Ouch. And yet, he persevered and became the sixteenth president of the United States.

You too can become the hero of your own story, no matter what obstacles you might be facing.

GROWTH ACTION

Become the hero of your story

1. Review the Hero's Journey; which stage are you at currently in your life?
2. What would a story of resilience look like?
3. What have you learned from your journey so far that you can use?
4. a) What might your story look like at:

   i) *The Abyss* stage?
   ii) *The Transformation* stage?
   iii) *The Hero's Return* stage?

   b) Take a moment to close your eyes and imagine yourself at each of these stages. How would it feel?

We all have our own battle to fight

Instead of asking, 'Why me?', you can ask 'What now?' and 'What would a story of resilience look like?' There is a Romanian saying my mother taught me, '*Toti ne caram crucea*', which means, '*We all have our own cross to carry*'. We all have to go through some form of suffering in this life. Romanians certainly know suffering, and fighting to survive, especially after decades of poverty, followed by a brutal communist dictatorship under Nicolae Ceauşescu which resulted in mass food shortages and abandoned children in orphanages, known as 'slaughterhouses of souls' for their despicable childhood abuse. In some cases, residents of Ceauşescu's regime even had no electricity or water. Eventually, civil war broke out between those loyal to the dictator, and those who wanted to overthrow the government and liberate it from his tyranny. It is no wonder that, in 1990, my parents fled Romania and came to the UK for safety and a better life, with just £100 in their back pocket. My grandfather actually told my father, 'Whatever you do ... don't come back. The secret police *will* kill you.'

Several years after settling into the UK, the Home Office tried to deport my family numerous times. I remember when I was only a few years old and my mum started crying on the phone. I didn't know what was happening, so I began crying too. My mother had just received a phone call to tell her that her final appeal to the Home Office had been rejected. She and my father had settled in the UK and they had a good quality of life. My mum worked three jobs, and my father was a tennis coach. They had a nice council house in a small town called Winford, not too far from Bristol Airport. I have some fond memories of playing in Winford, in the fields, in the forest, and in the mud.

Rather than give up, my parents decided they would put up a fight. And they fought *hard*; they got their neighbours to sign a petition, and managed to get the local MP and press on-board. The case eventually went to court – and they won! My mum said to me, however, 'If we got deported, we would have considered leaving you in the UK for a better life. Romania was *that* bad.'

What cross have you been asked to bear by life? We all have one to carry at some point. You can decide: 'I'm not going to carry this cross. It's too heavy. I don't see the point in carrying it any more!' Or, you can make a decision: 'I'm going to fight this out and be a hero!' That's exactly the decision I made. During my breakdown I remember obsessing over and over in my head: 'Why do I exist? What is existence?' I believe I had Existential OCD (Obsessive Compulsive Disorder) and had continuous obsessive thoughts about why I existed. I scared myself to death. I remember crying down the phone to my mum and saying, 'I can't live like this any more, Mum. I can't go on.' And she said to me, 'Nick, you're a *fighter*. You always have been, and always will be.' My mum has never trained as a coach, but her little pep talk worked. From that moment, I decided I was going to fight and emerge victorious. I would throw *everything* I had at recovering from my mental breakdown. So, I ended up going to therapy and 12-Step Recovery meetings weekly, practised deep relaxation regularly, and kept to a strict healthy diet which included no caffeine or alcohol.

None of these alone would have been the panacea. Medication alone would or could not fix me; you cannot make a plant well by just giving it super-fertiliser. Sadly, in our twenty-first-century world of quick fixes and instant gratification, many make the mistake thinking a pill will solve everything, without realising that medication needs to be part of a more holistic approach to mental health and thriving psychologically.

But all of what I did combined together? It was all very beneficial. Before long I was functional again. Why? Because my innate human needs were being met. My human need for connection and community was being met through 12-Step meetings and calls to fellows. My innate human need for purpose was also being met; I saw recovery from my mental breakdown as the challenge; I felt like someone who was told they would never walk again. All the various diagnoses I had received, from developmental PTSD, psychotic episode to generalised anxiety disorder with comorbid depression – I was determined I would overcome them all. And I did. It had its challenges, and was tough at times. But I became functional again. And if you're going through trauma right now, you can too with the right support! Of course, healing takes time. Be patient.

Starting a company is no easy feat; it's like getting punched in the face repeatedly, as it can be a journey riddled with rejections from customers, the market, legislation and investors. And you're expected to still smile at the end of the day. It is estimated 60 per cent of new businesses in the UK alone will go bust within their first three years.* Thus, it requires an extraordinary amount of resilience to create a thriving company. It can also require *huge* resilience and morale to get through life's challenges, whether it's a global pandemic, a mental health crisis, economic devastation, a major traumatic event, bereavement, war, and so forth. And the way to get through it all (without turning to drugs or alcohol) is to have a mission greater than one's self, one that transcends any pain and discomfort.

Comfortable, yet depressed

Despite my comforts and luxuries in London, I felt so ungrateful. *I should be happy or at least,* happier, I thought. Here I was moaning, living in an expensive Notting Hill flat and, at the end of the day, going to an equally expensive high-end health club and wallowing in self-pity in a warm jacuzzi.† There are much, much worse ways you could finish a day. I felt supremely ungrateful!

Alas, I cannot stress this enough: *money alone will not fulfil you, nor will it solve all your problems.* If this were true, then how come IMDB (Internet Movie Database) have a list they maintain of celebrities and actors who have died by suicide?‡ Having read through the list (which continues to grow year on year) as research for *The 7 Questions*, it was heartbreaking to see so many names, with so many talented souls, who simply could not bear

---

* The *Telegraph*, 'Start-ups across the UK are going bust – they need more careful management for our economy to boom'. https://www.telegraph.co.uk/politics/2019/01/24/start-ups-across-uk-going-bust-need-careful-management-economy/ – accessed 31 March 2021.
† They say money doesn't make you happy, and this is certainly true to an extent, though I'd much rather wallow in a jacuzzi with power jets.
‡ IMDB – Actors and Celebrities Who Committed Suicide: https://www.imdb.com/list/ls097007717/ – accessed 25 October 2020.

to live any more and felt it necessary to end their lives. In fact, when you do finally get the money, fame and recognition of your dreams, you too could well spiral into a depression. This rather reminds me of King Solomon, who reigned over Israel around 970 to 931 BCE. He was someone who had much wealth, land and lovers. And yet, in the end, he concluded in existential angst: 'Meaningless, meaningless! Everything is meaningless!' By *everything*, he was referring to his riches and worldly pleasures. While the exact extent of his wealth and sovereignty is a hotly debated issue among archaeologists, the lesson of wealth and pleasure alone not being fulfilling still stands, as I will demonstrate with some real-life case studies.

Alan was an extremely wealthy investor who was so successful he said he only had to work *one* day a month. The rest of the time, he would play tennis, go to the gym, and maybe do a bit of shopping for whatever he liked. He had already travelled the world, seen and done the things he wanted to do. And that was the problem: the world couldn't offer him anything any more. Thus, here he was on my sofa, complaining that he was now unhappy with his life. He acknowledged that most people would *dream* to be where he was. But money, and perhaps life itself, had become totally meaningless now that he had achieved and experienced all he wanted. What more could he experience exactly? Life had become but a pointless hedonistic treadmill for him.

A similar existential problem can also afflict successful entrepreneurs, those who achieve the dream: starting a company from scratch, and selling it for a humongous sum to an even bigger company. Notch (also known as Markus Persson) was a wildly successful game developer and founder of the video game Minecraft, which ended up being sold to Microsoft for $2.5 billion. Most founders would be ecstatic at having had their company acquired for that kind of money. But according to various news reports, Notch was allegedly 'depressed', 'unhappy' and 'melancholic' after the sale.*† He shared on social media, 'I've never felt more isolated' and 'the problem with getting everything is you run out of reasons to keep trying'. Solomon, Alan and Notch's cases do not surprise me at all; they had a meaning and purpose when they were striving towards something. But once they had climbed to the top of the mountain, while the view at first was spectacular, they had perhaps realised there was nowhere left to climb. All three of their predicaments come under what I call 'The Wile E. Coyote Effect'.

The Wile E. Coyote Effect

The Wile E. Coyote Effect is where one has lost the will to live after achieving one's ultimate goal in life. I named this phenomenon after a funny and apt clip from an episode of *Family Guy*. The clip humorously depicts cartoon character Wile E. Coyote finally catching the elusive Road Runner after many, many years. At first, Wile is ecstatic and he ends up celebrating by eating Road Runner with his dad. His dad asks him, 'What are you going to do next?' to which Wile replies, 'Huh, never really thought about it ... I've been chasing this damn bird for twenty years!'

A few weeks later, Wile is *still* sitting at the table, eating the last remnants of the Road Runner, looking a little bit glum and he begins drinking a beer. In the next scene, Wile is shown numbing out in front of a TV while drinking more heavily, looking dishevelled, slobbish and defeated as he repeatedly and mindlessly stares at the skull of his former nemesis, Road Runner. After having struggled in a brief stint working as a waiter to make ends meet, Wile ends up so depressed that he

---

* *New Zealand Herald*: https://www.nzherald.co.nz/entertainment/news/article.cfm?c_id=1501119&objectid=11506059 – accessed 3 October 2020.
† CNN: https://money.cnn.com/2015/08/31/technology/minecraft-creator-tweets/index.html – accessed 3 October 2020.

writes a suicide note ending with 'there's no reason to go on living', which he signs off with 'W.', before attempting to catapult himself into a wall. But don't worry, it has a happy ending which I won't spoil for you!

While hyperbolic and humorous (Wile E. is after all a cartoon character), it is also a surprisingly accurate depiction of what happens to human beings when they lose meaning and purpose; they develop an existential crisis, become depressed and, eventually, suicidal. Had I not found a solution to my existential crisis, perhaps I too would have also written my own note by now. Of course, the problem of purposelessness doesn't just affect the super-rich and super-accomplished – it can affect those who have been through much suffering and trauma. I have coached homeless people who have given up on life because of horrendous circumstances. However, comfort and motivation do not necessarily correlate.

You don't need to be comfortable to be motivated

There are soldiers who, despite facing gruelling training, being shot at occasionally or seeing friends die by their side, and enduring adverse weather conditions, all while carrying heavy field equipment and not being able to stop for a bite to eat, are *still* able to have the motivation to complete their mission and fulfil their duties. Even if you don't approve of war, one has to be in awe of how they are able to do it.

And what about entrepreneurs and company founders? I know from my own experience, in the early days, they may have a below minimum wage salary (if any at all), live on literally baked beans and orange juice for a while while crashing on a mattress on the floor in a friend of a friend's house (as I did), as well as facing countless and repeated rejections from prospective clients and investors, all for the mission of giving birth to a new business.

And then there were soldiers in the Second World War, many of whom *willingly* signed up (some even lying about their age or travelling thousands of miles back to the UK) to fight the Nazis, putting themselves in grave danger for a greater cause. Too often in the twenty-first century, with access to on-demand food, on-demand sex, all at the touch of a button, we have if anything learned to avoid (or medicate) pain at all costs and to prioritise individualism, materialism and hedonism. Despite personal challenges we may face, our generation has been more comfortable than any other.

We can overcome almost any suffering and pain if we have a purpose or a mission that is greater than ourselves. And if we don't, well, bad news: there is no pill that the doctor could prescribe you to help you find your life purpose. Antidepressants might make the pain more bearable, but they won't fix the existential hole. But the good news is that asking the right questions will. All I ask is for your patience as we navigate this process of finding what is meaningful and purposeful to you. In short, it's about finding someone, some people or a cause that you can devote yourself to. Maybe it's helping feed and clothe the homeless, perhaps it's doing pro bono work for vulnerable people, or maybe it's campaigning to stop professional organisations from ever using Comic Sans font – as long as it is a mission that is greater than yourself.

As one of the world's most prominent addiction recovery advocates and veterans, Russell Brand says in his book, *Recovery: Freedom From Our Addictions*, 'To be happy, I must have purpose.' This doesn't just apply to Brand; it applies to *every single human being* and is an innate human need. And often, it is not suffering that is intolerable, but suffering without a greater meaning. Thus, the purely reductionist and nihilistic view that we are mere meat machines that came from nothing, and will end up as nothing, in a world of seemingly pointless suffering, is no doubt a recipe for existential despair and depression. Thus, we need to think carefully about our existential beliefs and ask, 'Are my beliefs serving me?' It may even be necessary to *change* them.

Becoming willing to change your existential beliefs

When I was sixteen, I nearly had my first panic attack. I couldn't help but think about what would happen after I die. Would it just be endless silence and darkness for all eternity? The thought scared me so much that I almost wanted to run into my mum's room to ask if I could sleep in her bed!

I was always quite a deep thinker. When I was about thirteen years old, my mum and I went furniture shopping at IKEA. After reflecting on something I had learned in a physics class about cosmology, I asked her, 'Mum, what will happen when the sun runs out of hydrogen and then expands and engulfs the Earth in a few billion years' time?' Not exactly the kind of question you want to be answering on a Monday evening when you're tired after work. My mum scowled at me and snapped, 'Don't be stupid!' And that was that. Most likely, my mum was too busy worrying about work, bills, family stresses, which sofa to buy on a budget – you know, *normal* human problems. She didn't have time to be answering deep, scientific and existential questions from a thirteen-year-old! Alas, the existential thoughts around death didn't leave me, and I felt like the young Alvy Singer in the classic Woody Allen film, *Annie Hall*, where Singer's mother complains to the psychiatrist, Dr Flicker, 'He's so depressed ... he's even stopped doing his homework!' to which the young Alvy replies, 'What's the point? The universe is expanding and will eventually tear apart.' I felt terrified that at some point I had to face the eternal abyss. Once, I saw a documentary on TV that supposed one of two things will happen with the universe: either it will expand for ever (and possibly either freeze or just break apart), or it will stop expanding, and everything will be pulled back together creating a 'Big Crunch', and, quite possibly, another Big Bang. Why wasn't anyone else but me freaking out about this? This haunted me for some time as a teenager and I couldn't help thinking about death.

In my late twenties, I started to get really bad death anxiety after suffering several panic attacks. The thought wouldn't leave me, and it would scare me to death (no pun intended) whenever it crossed my mind. I would play video games, guitar, music, see my friends – anything to distract myself from the idea of mortality. My therapist questioned whether this fear was a form of narcissism. Quite possibly. After all, people die all the time, or to be more precise, nearly two people die every second on Earth. In the time you have just spent reading this, another two people have died. In the next twenty-four hours, another 43,000 people will be dead. Yet, guess whose death I am most worried about? My own, of course! How self-centred of me.

In life, we have to be willing to change ourselves – whether it's our ideas, values, attitude, lifestyle, beliefs, choices, priorities or actions – in order to change our lives. So, if you truly are dissatisfied in life, perhaps you may want to reconsider some of your values or beliefs. As a young man I was so certain I had life and everyone figured out: there is no point to life, the supernatural or the afterlife does not exist, Nirvana are the best band ever, long hair is a good look on me, committing to one person is a waste of time, as is sleep. However, as I got older, I began to see my beliefs were not only no longer serving me, but I might even be *wrong*. For example, we used to believe that the Earth was flat, and that the sun orbited the Earth. But we were later proved wrong by evidence. Similarly, doctors used to drain people of blood thinking that it would make them better (known as 'bloodletting'). Such practice, however, generally proved harmful (it turns out that we need blood to live!). Thus, we too should be open to changing our beliefs, whether they are scientific, psychological, or even existential.

We have so many beliefs and ideas. Many of us might say, 'I am not religious at all,' but how often do we cling to our own beliefs and ideas with absolute passion, certainty and tenacity? About anything and everything, from politics, which football team or TV show is best, to the meaning of life. We can also worship and can make gods out of our careers, money, possessions, physical appearances, sex, love, or external validation. But as both Western and Eastern philosophies teach, these are somewhat impermanent and, in the end, not enough to bring about lasting fulfilment (not all by themselves anyway). One of the great tools of CBC is the question: 'What's the consequences of this belief?' In other words, how does it *not* serve you?

Why we need to think about our beliefs around death

As someone who believes in Heaven, while I still fear death like most well-adjusted human beings, it doesn't give me the same terror as it once did, but more of a relief. For one, if life on Earth was a place to be reviewed on a travel site like TripAdvisor or Google Business, it would probably only have an average rating of 2/5, and would have plenty of reviews complaining they will *never* go there again, and that they demand to see the manager and get a refund. Right now, with my health intact, good finances, good friends, community, I'd probably give it a 4/5. But as an overall score? Probably 3/5. Thank goodness I don't have to stay here for ever or come back here again in its current state, especially with all the suffering in the world.

The afterlife, however, would have perfect review score, one that is simply not capable of being achieved here. Even the most luxurious hotels in the world do not have perfect ratings or reviews as far as I know – because anything created by humans on this planet will be imperfect, given our flawed natures.

If we are but meat machines or automatons with pre-programmed software (such as genes and innate needs) don't even machines have a set of optimal programming that will ensure they perform at their best? You could argue I'm taking a form of Pascal's Wager (which is if I'm wrong about the existence of Heaven there's no loss, but if I'm right I hit the afterlife jackpot), only I'm not taking the wager as an insurance policy for the afterlife. Rather, this is a variant, let's call it *Hatter's Wager*: believing there is an afterlife because it truly serves me best; it gives me hope for the future, more meaning and purpose, and stops me getting so agitated or upset about the little (or big) things in life and relieves me from any existential fear of death.

If you were staying in a bad two-star hotel for a short leg of your journey and you knew that shortly after you would be staying in a five-star hotel for the rest of your vacation, then, surely, you could probably manage a few days of discomfort? It would certainly give you hope and something to look forward to. How ludicrous it would be to be abandon the whole vacation just because there's a few bad days? For example, when I was flying to Australia for the first time, I had to endure thirty-six hours of flying from the UK. When I arrived in Australia, I was jet-lagged and spaced out and fatigued, and it took me a few days to recover. And while all of this was uncomfortable, I had a few weeks of beautiful Aussie weather and beaches to look forward to – so the temporary discomfort was worth it. So, if you're going through a bad period in your life, believing in Heaven can be very beneficial; in the context of eternity, your life is barely a small speck of time, and that bad period, likewise, will not last for ever. If you believe in this existential model of the afterlife, then suffering becomes more tolerable. Why? Because you have hope for a better future. And hope gives us energy to keep going and is a fundamental need.

My godmother, Joan, once told me about how her grandmother's final words on her deathbed were, 'Do not cry for me, child, for I am returning home!' What a beautiful way to die. Hearing these words moved me profoundly. Joan's grandmother was able to die peacefully because of her beliefs, which gave her (and Joan) great hope for the future.

Of course, it would also be fair to ask, 'So why not just kill yourself if there is a Heaven?' Well, if there is a Heaven, then there must be a god of some sort, which means your life on Earth has meaning, and you were created for a specific reason and purpose. To quote Mark Twain: 'The two most important days in your life are the day you are born and the day you find out why.' But talking about 'God' can sometimes, for many reasons, make people irritated.

Resistance to 'the G word'

To quote Alcoholics Anonymous's Big Book:

> With ministers, and the world's religions, I parted right there. When they talked of a God personal to me, who was love, superhuman strength and direction, I became irritated and my mind snapped shut against such a theory.

I have noticed that even in collegial discussions around existential beliefs that people can get very heated – especially if the word 'God' is involved. Take it from me, as someone who used to be vehemently anti-religious. It's just a concept; how can there be so much emotion and anger? You probably wouldn't get the same level of reaction if you were discussing cats or trees (although, then again, humans are capable of fighting about anything, especially on the internet). Some other reasons for people getting angry when the 'G word' comes up may include:

- Existential anger; if someone is actively going through or has gone through a lot of pain and trauma, trying to tell them that there's an all-powerful, all-knowing and

all-loving God who loves them may understandably
cause them to get angry

- Wanting to protect belief systems that form part of
  their identity (self-preservation)
- Negative associations of God with aggressive or
  judgemental preachers ('You'll burn in hell!') or holier-
  than-thou believers, dogma, brainwashing, extremism
  (ISIS, Westboro Baptist Church, inquisitions, witch-
  burning, cults, crusades), homophobia, church
  misconduct (abuse committed by corrupt priests,
  misusing funds raised solely for personal gain,
  exclusion of certain groups)
- Not wanting to feel beholden or accountable to
  a parental-like figure, or feeling like you're being
  watched or judged
- Possible pattern match of the word 'God' in the
  amygdala to parents (unconsciously), which can trigger
  resentment if the parents were abusive or absent
- Don't want to be told they're not at the top of the
  power or intellectual pyramid (this can be a humbling
  experience, which the ego does not like)
- Have a conception of God being tyrannical,
  judgemental, vengeful, angry, unforgiving, or damning

Looking back at my old existential beliefs, I can see how all
of these applied to me. In any case, when considering the various possibilities of an afterlife, and the meaning of life itself,
it's certainly hard to avoid 'the G word', as for many centuries,
humans have looked to the supernatural for answers.

The downside of believing in God

Psychologists and psychotherapists point to the good that can
come out of religious communities as well as belief in God.

Acclaimed psychologist and former president of the American Psychological Association (APA), Dr Martin Seligman, also links belief in God to positive mental health:[*]

> One truth about meaning is this: the larger the entity to which you can attach yourself, the more meaning you will feel your life has. While some argue that generations that lived for God ... were misguided, these same generations surely felt their lives imbued with meaning. The individual, the consuming self, isolated from larger entities, is a very poor site for a meaningful life. However, the bloated self is fertile soil for the growth of depression.

Indeed, being overly self-centred can be a recipe for depression as we explored earlier in this book. However, there can be a downside to believing in God too – if you conceive God to be a control freak, vengeful, angry, unforgiving and uncaring, then such a belief may actually be *harming* and not helping you. For example, one of my friends, who is a clinical psychologist, said that she had treated people with Religious OCD – a type of OCD where people become obsessive and excessively fearful of God, and engage in compulsive religious rituals. This can be a type of existential anxiety, one where they feel God is waiting for them to trip up and to punish them accordingly – unless they do the rituals. Another client of hers felt ashamed because he was homosexual and believed God was ashamed of him as a result.[†] Certain groups and communities have certainly been persecuted, shunned, shamed and abandoned by

---

[*] Martin E. P. Seligman, PhD, *The Optimistic Child – A Proven Programme to Safeguard Children Against Depression and Build Lifelong Resilience* (Boston: Houghton Mifflin, 2007), 42.
[†] There's a great TED talk by Kristin Saylor and Jim O'Hanlon on whether or not homosexuality is actually 'a sin' – see https://www.youtube.com/watch?v=XGNZQ64xiqo.

various religious organisations, which are created and run by *humans*. As a result, there's a 'human tendency to bugger up', as vicar and author John Peters puts it. So perhaps it's not God (if they exist) who alienates us, but rather, *we* alienate people from God, through various forms of preachiness, insensitivity, hatred, judgement and intolerance.

If you do believe in God, another common and difficult question you might be asked, or even ask yourself is, 'Why did God allow this to happen?' It is challenging to keep belief in God when you see starving, sick or dying people, especially where their deaths could be prevented. However, a lot of hunger and poverty isn't caused by bad weather, but rather, by human greed and corruption. We humans could certainly relocate people living in places that are most hazardous to life and distribute resources more fairly. Yet, some of us (even those of us who are believers) point the finger and blame God.

This very question ('Why God, *why?*') can sometimes lead to existential despair in believers. One of my previous counsellors, Jennifer Garland, a therapist based in Missouri, US, had such despair herself when she suffered a miscarriage in 2006. As a devoted Christian, it sent her spiralling into a clinical depression. She simply could not understand why on earth a loving God would have permitted this to happen to her, a faithful and committed Christian. In Jennifer's case, she eventually managed to come out of her depression, and later down the line, she happened to meet another woman who had the same thing happen to her. After meeting this woman, Jennifer was convinced that God allowed her to go through this trial of suffering so that she would know how to help others in a similar situation, and now her faith (and mental health) is stronger than ever. Thus, belief in God is most likely beneficial only if you perceive God to be wise and loving, rather than tyrannical and malevolent. Otherwise, it's most likely going to do more harm than good.

Beware of the Backfire Effect

A lot of people may say they are 'open to evidence'. But are they really? Because of unconscious biases, we may reject evidence or logic, even if it is plausible or credible. For example, we can be victims of 'confirmation bias'; interpreting, accepting or discarding only information that confirms previously held beliefs. Another phenomenon to be aware of is the 'Backfire Effect', where trying to argue with someone who has a strongly held belief can sometimes only reinforce it. For example, as a non-follower of football, I once argued (albeit naively) with Bristol Rovers Football Club fans that Bristol City FC was *objectively* the more skilled team (because they were several divisions higher at the time). In UK football, the more skilled and able your team, then the higher the division they will play in. It's that simple. This logic, of course, was met with lots of resistance (and a few insults!). Clearly, as human beings, we can be very loyal to a tribe or an ideology, even in the face of conflicting evidence. Thus, arguing with a believer in certain football teams, political parties, existential beliefs or whether pineapple on pizza is a crime,* can further entrench them in their views. It should be noted as well that humans will *literally* have a fight or go to war over their beliefs.

Therefore, when interrogating and challenging your own beliefs, remember that you too may be clinging hard to certain ideologies and you may experience resistance from your own ego! With some of your bigger beliefs, why not try fostering a sense of curiosity? What might it feel like, just for one day, to believe something different? How might it feel to 'act as if'? To quote an often-used saying from executive coaching: *what got you here, won't get you there.*

---

* You will never convince me that this is wrong.

In a nutshell

Our beliefs, both psychological and existential, shape our reality and play a very important part in our mental health and well-being, as shown by various psychology studies and demonstrated by my own personal stories. If after reading this chapter, you realise that your beliefs might not be serving you, whether they are psychological or existential, here's some general guidance for you:

- Ask yourself, 'How can I act "as if"?' and use your imagination to rehearse a new response
- Keep asking questions, such as:
  - Is this belief really true?
  - Is this belief really my own?
  - How did I form this belief?
  - What evidence is there against this?
- Some beliefs are created as a result of deeply emotional events and may require professional help from a life coach, a therapist, guided imagery or hypnosis in order to be untangled or reprogrammed – pure cognitive approaches are often not enough for beliefs created from trauma or strong emotional experiences, such as with phobias.
- Keep an open mind and ask yourself, 'Am I biased towards or prejudiced against a certain answer?' For example, in the UK courts, jurors have to disclose anything that might prejudice the decision, such as if they know the defendant personally. Perhaps there are reasons that may likewise cause you to reach certain conclusions or to see any counter-logic or evidence through a certain lens.
- Follow the evidence wherever it may lead and be willing to be wrong (something our ego *hates*),

remembering that even scientific research, theories
and models can be later shown to be incorrect, just as
previously widely accepted medical and psychological
'treatments' have later been shown to be harmful. We
are always learning as a human race.

- Remember that many decisions are made in faith, even
those made in the courtroom on logic and evidence,
and that faith is a choice.

In the materialistic West, many of us have become too comfortable and too worldly. We can at times be like King Xerxes,
from the film *300*, who arrogantly believes he is a deity because
of his towering height, his wealth and the size of his army.
However, when Leonidas, the king of the Spartans, throws a
spear that cuts Xerxes' cheek and causes him to bleed, Xerxes
is traumatised and touches his cheek in horror, realising he is
not the immortal god he thought he was. Likewise, many of us
forget our mortality and this is shown by our complacency in
life, our ability to procrastinate, to care too much about trivial
or superficial matters, and so forth. Many of us see suffering on
the news, and we can unconsciously think, 'that will happen
to other people, but not me'. But some of us know too well
tragedies can indeed happen to us or those we care about. We
need to be able to make sense of suffering, because when the
storm of suffering comes (and it's a question of not *if*, but *when*),
we need to be prepared. At some point we *will* suffer, whether
it's the loss of a job, a loved one or a relationship, illness, a
catastrophic diagnosis, a traumatic event, the infirmities of our
body as we age, the unexpected onslaught of annoying music at
3 a.m., or your favourite football team losing. Regardless of what
you believe, everything is temporary, including our own life on
Earth. We need to be able to make sense of such suffering, or
else we may become very depressed. And to be able to make
sense of suffering requires us to look at our existential beliefs.

If you want to, you can believe that the life we have is all there is, and that there is no ultimate meaning to life or suffering. The question is: which belief(s) will serve you best? Are you sure your beliefs are serving you? I will leave this as an exercise for you to ponder. After all, our beliefs can, as explained in this chapter, influence how much meaning, purpose, hope and self-esteem we have. Remember not to cling too tightly to your beliefs and to be aware of biases you may have in trying to change those beliefs (similar to how low self-esteem makes us unconsciously biased against ourselves).

CHAPTER 7

What's the Next
Smallest Step I Can Take?

*'Sometimes the smallest step in the right
direction ends up being the biggest step of your
life. Tiptoe if you must, but take a step.'*

—NAEEM CALLAWAY

'What's the next smallest step I can take?' is very effective for incisively cutting through all the noise in your head about what to do next. It's so simple that it's almost common sense. But again: common sense is not always common practice.

Change can be liberating and exciting, but it can also be overwhelming and stressful – even if it's positive. The process of change can certainly bring up all kinds of discomfort in us, which leads us to procrastinate. Procrastination is a bit like hiking and stumbling across a huge mountain in your path and thinking, *There's no way can I climb* that, *it's way too high and too much work! I think I'll leave it for another day.* The problem is, you need to climb the mountain to get where you're going. And the longer you put off climbing it, the more painful it becomes, especially as your supplies start to dwindle, and you become more fatigued.

One piece of advice I had from a university lecturer was when writing a new assignment, just start by creating a new document, giving it a title, and then saving it. If you manage to do that, great, you're already one step closer to finishing it! Perhaps the next step, if you're feeling brave, is to start writing the first sentence. If you can do that, then perhaps you might want to just finish writing the first paragraph. Before you know it, you've got a snowball of momentum. But the hardest step? It's often the first one.

Perfection is the enemy of progress

Procrastinating on starting and finishing

At times, when I was writing this book, I found myself getting stuck, and losing momentum. And often that 'stuckness' was because of procrastination's best friend, perfection, who said:

> *Hi Nick! Your writing has to be totally perfect, or there's no point in writing at all. You might as well not bother.*
>
> *Yours sincerely,*
> *Perfection (your nemesis)*

In your own life, think about where this voice of toxic perfectionism has crept in. Perhaps you too are considering writing a book, creating your own video channel, starting a business, but that big idea still hasn't become a reality just yet. If so, it's quite possible that it's because you're seeing the mountain and are feeling overwhelmed at the prospect of climbing it. Or perhaps you're thinking you have to do everything 100 per cent perfectly, and thus, you're falling into analysis paralysis, or the trap of thinking, *I either do it perfectly or not at all.* The way to break through all this is to just take the tiniest step possible – no matter how small.

When it comes to big projects, doing a little each day is best to keep up the momentum. One of my clients, Peter, was an author with some pretty bad writer's block. After exploring why, we realised that he was procrastinating – and surprise, surprise – it was due to perfectionism. He didn't want to face the discomfort of producing something potentially mediocre. In his mind, it had to be an absolute masterpiece. So, I challenged him to send me the 'SFD' (shitty first draft) of his outline by next week. I also did some guided hypnosis with him, where we got him to visualise doing the work and letting the words just flow out of him unfiltered. Within a week, sure enough, he had got it done – and then some! And thereafter, he was able to break through his inertia and make some serious progress on his project.

Procrastinating exercising

Sometimes, I find that same voice of toxic perfectionism saying the same thing about my workouts too:

> *Hi Nick! Your nemesis here again. Your workout has to be one hour of hardcore and intense exercise – or else there's no point doing it. Seeing as you don't feel totally energised today, you might as well just laze on the couch and do nothing.*
>
> *Yours sincerely,*
> *Perfection*

In an interview with one of the world's leading sports nutrition brands, *MyProtein*, I shared about how some days in my weight loss journey, I *really* didn't feel up to a full workout. The perfectionist in me said, 'See? There's no point going to the gym.' Instead, I would ask myself, 'What's the next smallest step

I could take?' Sometimes, the answer would be just getting on a cross-trainer for ten minutes, or going for a short walk, and that was it. As a result of this strategy, combined with a balanced diet, and good rest, I was able to drop over 10 per cent body fat and 22 kg in the space of a year! You're not always going to feel up to a killer of a workout. So just do what you can with the energy and the time that you do have. If you think that each workout needs to end up with you totally breathless, dripping with sweat and exhausted, then it's no wonder that you'll procrastinate; just merely thinking about it will be enough to deter you! Take the pressure off yourself to perform at 100 per cent effort each workout. And note that if you're past your thirties or forties, or if you have a chronic condition such as arthritis, chronic fatigue or fibromyalgia, you likely won't have the same stamina you had when you were younger. Similarly, if you've been physically inactive for a while, it will take some time to get yourself moving, develop a good routine and to re-sculpt your physique. So be realistic and patient with yourself.

Change can be stressful

If you ask counsellors and psychologists the definition of stress, they may well say: *change.* The psychiatrists Thomas Holmes and Richard Rahe came up with the Social Readjustment Rating Scale after surveying five thousand medical patients to see if stress was related to illness. Patients were asked to tally a list of forty-three life events based on a relative score, and a positive correlation was found between their life events and their illnesses.

The more life change units someone accumulates, the more likely it is they will be stressed, and then become ill. We are creatures of habit, and even positive changes (such as getting married, or achieving something huge) can sometimes be stressful. The amount of stress they could cause for us is shown in

Table 1 in terms of Life Change Units. When we have to adapt to change, our brains must work a bit harder to keep up. For example, becoming hugely successful, to the extent of near or actual celebrity status, will put you further in the limelight. For some, this can be positive and desirable, but it can also be fear-inducing, and you may have to adapt to the amount of attention from people and the media you receive, as well as being more careful what you say in public. I for one have had to exercise more caution myself, now as a published author! Getting married, while a positive experience, can also bring about stress. For example, the logistics of organising the wedding, of merging finances and resources, as well as potentially looking at the possibility of never dating anyone new again ('til death do you part!).

Eventually, we do find our 'groove' and we can 'settle in' again, and we won't have to think as hard or problem-solve any more. In any case, if you are looking to change your life, it is better to start small. You can also use the power of your imagination to visualise what positive change would look like (which we'll explore later in this chapter).

Table 1: Some life changes that could be stressful (from Holmes and Rahe, 1967)

Life event	Life change units
Marriage	50
Change in financial state	38
Change to different line of work	36
Outstanding personal achievement	28
Beginning or ending school	26

Life event	Life change units
Change in living conditions	25
Change in working hours or conditions	20
Change in residence	20
Change in social activities	18
Change in sleeping habits	16
Change in eating habits	15
Change in WiFi availability*	9,000+

Change can be scary

Whether you are trapped in a corporate job or an unfulfilling relationship, it can be scary to imagine a different life. For example, a life without a stable and comfortable salary (such as before you launch that business or get your big break). Or a life without your current partner, or, even more terrifyingly, a life without coffee or chocolate![†] *Sometimes the most comfortable prisons are the hardest to escape.* You may fear things will not work out, or fear that you're not good enough to make that future change possible. But here's the good news: you don't need to leave your job (or your partner) tomorrow. You only need to take the next smallest step. That could be doing your research, having that key conversation, or perhaps abstaining from coffee or chocolate *just for today*. It's true that to beat addictions, radical action is necessary. But when it comes to beating procrastination, *less is more*. Here's a poem to remember:

---

* Wasn't part of Holmes and Rahe's original life events scale, but a loss of WiFi connection can be stressful especially in a post coronavirus world!

† Many would struggle to live without either of these, but it could be something else you could not bear to be without!

Done is better than perfect,
Some is better than done,
And a little is better than none!

When you can take the smallest step, it's often easier to take the next one because you can say to yourself, 'See? That wasn't so bad!' And then take another. A tiny push of a snowball down-hill can be all it takes to create an avalanche of momentum! For example, I can procrastinate doing washing up. I really hate it. But what I found helpful is to say, 'OK, I will wash up just *one* fork.' Forks are easy to clean, and they are the least gross. Often when I have washed that one fork, I might then wash another. And another. And before I know it, all the washing up is done!

You only need to take that first tiny step, and then have *faith* that the rest of the steps will naturally follow. Faith doesn't necessarily make things easier, but it does make them *possible.* So instead of asking yourself, 'What if it goes wrong?' or 'What if I can't do it?', try asking instead, 'What if it *does* work out?' If you're fearful of what others may think of this change you're about to make, remember one of the most common dying regrets: 'I wish I'd had the courage to live a life true to myself, not the life others expected of me.'

Of course, sometimes the fear of change can be so intense that it may in fact be because of *trauma.*

Sometimes trauma is the enemy

I had a client, Rick, a promising actor in his late twenties. He had every area in his life down. Finances? Check. Career? Check. Friendships? Check. But relationships? Not at all. Talking to a woman would make him freeze like a deer in the headlights. I tried all sorts of cognitive coaching approaches, but when he went off to speed dating, he told me he 'bottled it'. He couldn't speak to even one woman because he was so anxious. In our sessions, I observed his response seemed 'phobic'. When I suggested he could be suffering from *gynophobia* (fear of women), it really resonated with him. We can develop phobias of anything or anyone, and they can be created as a result of a traumatic event. When trauma is involved, a different approach is needed – ideally a hypnotic one. I asked if he remembered any events involving women, and he recalled one involving a rejection as a teenager where he was humiliated. His amygdala was thus pattern matching to that event, so that speaking to a woman would cause it to sound the alarm and pump out adrenaline, pushing him into a flight/freeze response, which would explain his quite literal 'freezing up'. In order to overcome this, we would need to put him into a relaxed state and then reprocess the original traumatic event, such that the cortisol (stress) is removed from the memory, and it becomes like any other memory. This is, in essence, what the Rewind technique does. Afterwards, we then did some guided hypnosis where we had him imagine going to a speed-dating event feeling really calm, confident and relaxed. The results of all this were unbelievable. A few days later, I received a text message from Rick, saying: 'Went to speed dating – and I managed to speak to seventeen women. I was pretty nervous though!' I was amazed. I jokingly reminded him that only *psychopaths* don't feel any nervousness in social situations, and asked him if he wanted to be one (he said no, thankfully!).

Rick was procrastinating talking to women, not because he was lazy, or he wasn't brave, but because he was *traumatised*. Similarly, in your life, if there's something you absolutely dread doing (and it fills you with terrible anxiety when you try to do it), whether it's going outside, driving a car, or even giving a presentation, then it might be more than mere procrastination, but could be trauma. In this case, the next smallest step might be seeking out a trained professional who can help with phobias and trauma.

Motivating yourself for change

Most likely, if you're reading this book, you actually want to change your life, right? Whether it's finding more fulfilment, contentment, meaning, purpose, or something more extrinsic such as increasing your annual earnings, losing some weight, or even gaining some muscle. Thus, let's consider the *Gleicher-Dannemiller Formula for Change*:

Change = D $\times$ V $\times$ F > R

Where
D = Dissatisfaction
V = Vision of what is possible
F = First concrete steps towards the vision
R = Resistance to change

Now, if all of these factors are greater than your resistance to change, you will change! But if your resistance to change is greater, then you will rebel, and change will not happen. How do we further overcome resistance? You also need humility, open-mindedness and willingness, as well as a longer-term plan. Thus, let's change this formula to become the *Hatter Formula for Change*:

Change = D $\times$ V $\times$ H $\times$ O $\times$ W $\times$ (F + S)

Where
D = Dissatisfaction
V = Vision of what is possible
H = Humility
O = Open-mindedness to new ideas and information
W = Willingness to choose differently and commit
   to change

F = First tiny steps towards the vision
S = Strategy

Someone with severe alcoholism or a drug problem who has lost their home, their family and their job as a result of their addiction is much more likely to have a higher D (Dissatisfaction) value. Likewise, so is someone who has eaten so many sugary foods that they have developed type 2 diabetes. In recovery, we would call this 'hitting rock bottom'.

H, O, W *and* S are also essential components:

- *Humility (H)* is the ability to accept that one might be wrong and not have all the answers;
- *Open-mindedness (O)* is how receptive you are to any new information;
- *Willingness (W)* to choose differently and committing to the process of change is also key; and
- *Strategy (S)* is needed for longer-term momentum, anticipating obstacles and how you will overcome them.

Without these components, you can be dissatisfied with life, and even dream of a better future, and maybe even have a vague plan. But if you're not humble enough to perhaps seek some outside help, to be open to trying something new or willing to make some different choices, then your dissatisfaction and blue-sky vision of a better you are, in a word, useless. But if you become humble and seek some help (such as from a book, a mentor, a coach, or a therapist), and you become open-minded (such as to the questions, suggestions, analogies and perspectives in this book) and you are willing to try something new, your chance of changing will become so much greater.

I once worked with an accomplished businesswoman in her fifties, who seemed a bit cantankerous and rigid. On our initial consultation, she told me rather bluntly, 'I have had three successful businesses. I'm in my fifties and I've been around the block a few times in life. So, frankly, I don't see what you can teach me that is new.' I quietly despaired when I heard this. Even if her D and V values were high, her H and O values sounded very low. In as tactful terms as I could muster, and with self-control and professionalism, I tried to gently explain, 'Without humility ... I'm afraid coaching doesn't work.' Sometimes it's more powerful to let the client come to the answer themselves. But equally, in coaching, sometimes you have to be willing to break rapport in order to help your client and 'give it to them straight'. And the issue is that the truth can be harsh and disturbing, and it can shatter how we perceive ourselves, and crack our fragile egos. But sometimes, ego reduction is exactly what we need in order to mature and grow as human beings.

GROWTH ACTION

Apply the Change Formula

$$CHANGE = D \times V \times H \times O \times W \times (F + P)$$

Reflective questions

1. **D = Dissatisfaction**

   What challenges do I have – and what are the costs and consequences of having these?

2. **V = Vision of what is possible**

   What would life be like if I could overcome these challenges? What positive changes would I see/feel/experience if I could overcome these challenges? How might my life benefit?

3. **H = Humility**

   How have I failed overcoming this all by myself? What led me to needing to seek out help? What have I already tried to overcome this?

4. **O = Open-mindedness to new ideas and information**

   How open am I to new ideas, suggestions, and perspectives?

   What do I need to change in myself in order to become more open?

5. **W = Willingness to choose differently and commit**

   Am I willing to go to any lengths to change? How willing I am to implement agreed action plans or suggestions?

6. **F = First concrete steps towards the vision**

   What are the very first tiny steps to overcoming this challenge, no matter how small?

7. **P = Plan of action and strategy**

   What's my plan of action? What's my longer-term strategy?

   What obstacles might there be along the way and how might I overcome them?

Actually taking the next step

Turn your 'I can' and 'should' into 'I will'

When my clients say, 'I'll try to do it', or 'I should do it', I call them out on it. 'Try to' implies subconsciously that they haven't *really* committed to doing it. Can you imagine if you called an ambulance and they said, 'We'll *try* to send an ambulance over.' You would probably ask, 'Wait, what do you mean "try"? I'm having a heart attack here!' Or, if you ordered food at a restaurant, and were told, 'We'll *try* to prepare your food.' This wouldn't instil you with much confidence either! Now compare it with 'We *will* send an ambulance over,' and 'We *will* prepare your food.' Notice how the latter sounds so much more definite and certain that it's going to happen. One NLP staple is that the language we use with ourselves (and others) can affect behaviour. Self-talk can certainly make a difference, from my own, and my clients' experiences.

Thus, once you've determined the next smallest step you can take, the next thing to do is to *commit*: what *will* you do next?

Take the first smallest step – *right now*

Nowadays, limited companies can be incorporated almost instantly online. New books can be started by simply opening your word processor software and saving it with a new document name. Emails can be sent instantaneously. Applications can be made online without you even having to leave your house. Whatever that first step is, let me ask you: is it possible to take that smallest step *right now*? If so, go and do it this moment. Put down this book, do it, then come back. Literally do just ten minutes and no more.

*Take that smallest step **right now**.*

When you have done so, continue reading.

So, did you do it yet? If not, what *really* stopped you? OK, if you're on your commute home, or on the toilet – fair enough. But what's stopping you doing it when you get straight home or after you've washed your hands? What do you need to change in order to do it?

If you're still procrastinating even doing the smallest step, then you need to ask yourself:

- Is this *really* the smallest possible step?
- Is the vision of taking the step compelling enough?
- Are the consequences of *not* doing it clear?
- Am I running from anything?

Overwhelm and stress can stop us

Sometimes, we can feel so overwhelmed and stressed that the idea of taking that first step stresses us out – especially if it might cause some changes. If you're not getting your fundamental needs met, then you might not have enough 'spare capacity' psychologically to stretch yourself further (and I recommend you take the Emotional Needs Audit in Chapter 2). If you are stressed or highly anxious, you will be hijacked by your amygdala and you will struggle to think clearly. Note that when you are stressed, you are likely to succumb to cognitive distortions, such as making a mountain out of a molehill, thus making even that next smallest step seem like huge effort! You might also be stressed because you're harbouring some hidden resentment, fear or shame, in which case, refer back to Chapter 3 ('Am I Running From Anything?'), and use some of the self-coaching questions I laid out. If you're still procrastinating, perhaps you just need a bit of relaxation so that you can gather some clarity about the next smallest step, and have enough spare capacity psychologically and physically to take it. For example, if you were thirsting for water after three days of being dehydrated, how motivated would you be to learn complex algebra? Probably not motivated at all. Likewise, sometimes, we need to relax, and get our fundamental needs met first.

Relax and win

There was once a princess who was riding on a horse when suddenly her tiara fell off her head into a big muddy lake. That tiara was very precious and expensive, so she began frantically and desperately looking for it, and in doing so, muddied her beautiful white dress. When she couldn't find it, she became incredibly distressed and started crying out to her servants and guards, who also joined in the search. Of course, at this point, all of the mud, dirt and debris at the bottom of the lake was now being kicked up, making the water murky and choppy. Luckily, it just so happened there was a wise old man walking past. The princess saw him and asked for help. So, the wise old man told everyone to stop looking for a moment. The princess and the servants looked confused, but they did as the wise man suggested anyway. After everyone had stopped splashing around, the princess could see through the lake much more clearly. And lo and behold, she was finally able to find her tiara, which she plucked out of the water. She was amazed at how simple the solution had been; all she had to do was let the debris and the waves settle so she could see more clearly.

When we are stressed or highly emotionally aroused, our amygdala takes over our thinking and feeling, shutting us off from our pre-frontal cortex (thinking brain). Our thinking and feeling can then become *very* distorted. Thus, procrastinating, whether it's binge-watching TV or falling into the social media scroll-hole, may seem like a good idea at the time in our distorted-thinking state. In some cases, before I can do any meaningful coaching with someone, it can be necessary to first put them into a state of deep relaxation using guided imagery. After making them deeply relaxed, they often feel much calmer and can think much more clearly. I have had clients experience a rapid transformation after just *one* session because of guided deep relaxation. In the next session, they come back and tell me that they are falling asleep faster and easier, and generally look a bit younger, brighter, have much more energy and feel better.

One of the best things you can do if you suffer from anxiety, depression, stress or insomnia is regular relaxation. You can, in a word, literally relax your way to a better life. Sleep is of course vital for general mental health; if we haven't slept well or for long enough, we can be more anxious, moody, emotional and lethargic, because our nervous system hasn't had a proper chance to discharge emotional arousal from the day before.

Many people try to relax with meditation, however, if you're like me and you feel like jumping out of your skin when you try to do it, then you may be one of many who really struggle with it. There are some good guided meditation apps out there to help (such as Calm and Headspace), which can be a bit easier to meditate with than trying to meditate unaided. However, from my experience, those with a lot of trauma can feel really uncomfortable with meditation, as to sit with thoughts and feelings, especially if they're traumatic, can cause severe anxiety and distress. Thus, guided hypnosis can be a more comfortable and easier option for many. In fact, I've had clients get so relaxed from me doing guided hypnosis they have fallen asleep in the session! You need not do anything except relax and just follow the suggestions in guided hypnosis. And as you do so, you may find yourself becoming more relaxed ... as you drift deeper into relaxation ... even if the mind feels busy ... you may notice how it begins to slow down ... and feel quieter ... that's it ... because you may find ... guided relaxation can be *very* relaxing ... and requires very little effort ... when done with a soothing voice ... and you may find yourself ... breathing deeper and slower ... which helps you to relax even deeper ...

Some may try to 'relax' with exercise, and though exercise can be cathartic and help you sleep better, as well as boost serotonin ('happiness hormone') levels, it also fires up the nervous system. It's not the same as the 'relaxation response' (known as the 'rest and digest response') for your nervous system. Note that if you're struggling to have the energy to exercise, it could be because stress and anxiety are consuming a lot of energy in the brain (which is an energy-guzzling organ!) as well as affecting the amount and quality of sleep you get. So again, the best thing you can do is to relax more, and you may find that your energy gets restored.

Finally, one of the most miraculous things about activating the relaxation response (such as through deep breathing, guided hypnosis or meditation) is that researchers have discovered that the body can start repairing itself at a cellular level with just fifteen minutes of relaxation!* So regular relaxation is not only great for mental health, but it could also help you to be more physically healthy – and live longer. And, of course, improved sleep quality will help your body get more deep sleep, which is when the body does vital physical repair and maintenance. Many hard-working and driven people (workaholics especially) can think of sleep and relaxation as a waste of time. But as shown by much emerging research, not only is sleep for winners, but so is relaxation too. Being relaxed can make you more

---

* M. K. Bhasin, J. A. Dusek, B. H. Chang, M. G. Joseph, J. W. Denninger, *et al.*, 'Relaxation Response Induces Temporal Transcriptome Changes in Energy Metabolism, Insulin Secretion and Inflammatory Pathways', *PLOS ONE* 8:5(2013), e62817. https://doi.org/10.1371/journal.pone.0062817.

creative* – and it is creativity that leads to 'a-ha!' moments in art, problem-solving, innovation and game-changing inventions that can transform businesses and even the world. Certainly, in my own life, my best business ideas, such as giftgaming and FDBK, have come when I felt relaxed and playful. To quote Albert Einstein: 'Creativity is the residue of time wasted.'

Imagining your way to success

Guided relaxation isn't the only application of mental rehearsal. What is 'mental rehearsal'? Mental rehearsal is where you rehearse something in your imagination, such as with hypnosis. It's where you or a practitioner guides your imagination and allows you to experience something as if it was actually happening, such as feeling confident in presentations or interviews, being assertive, going to bed at a regular time, or even running faster!

In the dystopian sci-fi film, *The Matrix*, the protagonist, Neo, learns how to fight by having his mind connected to a virtual reality simulator. Once the simulation is set up, he begins furiously sparring in a virtual dojo with his aide and mentor, Morpheus. When the simulation comes to an end, he awakes from the simulator and the first thing he says is, 'I know kung fu.' While *The Matrix* is, of course, pure sci-fi, mental rehearsal is not. When we have practised something in our mind, it can be easier and more natural to do it in real life – because we create false memories of having done it; new neural pathways are created, and we develop a sort of mental 'muscle memory'.

To demonstrate the effectiveness of mental rehearsal, a study carried out by the Cleveland Clinic Foundation in Ohio, US, took thirty young healthy people and split them into three

---

* Ding Xiaoqian, Yi-Yuan Tang, Rongxiang Tang and Michael Posner, 'Improving creativity performance by short-term meditation', *Behavioral and Brain Functions*, 10: 9 (2014). https://doi.org/10.1186/1744-9081-10-9.

groups: Group #1 mentally rehearsed exercising their little finger; Group #2 mentally rehearsed exercising their biceps; and Group #3 did no exercise, acting as a control group. The strengths of each group were measured before and after – and the results were phenomenal:

- Group #1 had increased their finger strength by **35 per cent**
- Group #2 increased biceps strength by **13.5 per cent** (and maintained that gain for *three months* after training had stopped)
- Group #3 (who did no mental rehearsal), saw no significant strength increases[*]

So, you could say, Groups #1 and #2 increased their strength literally without lifting a finger and using only their imagination! Other studies carried out by sports psychologists have also shown basketball players were able to improve their shooting accuracy (as well as their mental state during taking shots) using mental rehearsal alone.[†‡] In addition, there are numerous studies reporting how therapists have been successfully using mental rehearsal to help clients overcome phobias and OCD.[§]

---

[*] V. K. Ranganathan, V. Siemionow, J. Z. Liu, V. Sahgal and G. H. Yue, 'From mental power to muscle power – gaining strength by using the mind', *Neuropsychologia*, 42:7 (2004), 944–956. https://doi.org/10.1016/j.neuropsychologia.2003.11.018.

[†] J. Pates, A. Cummings and I. Maynard, 'The effects of hypnosis on flow states and three-point shooting performance in basketball players', *Sport Psychologist*, 16:1(2002), 34–47. https://dx.doi.org/10.1123/tsp.16.1.34.

[‡] Jamaal Edward Cannon, 'Effects of imagery use in basketball free throw shooting,' Theses Digitization Project (2008), 3354. https://scholarworks.lib.csusb.edu/etd-project/3354.

[§] Kathleen (Kate) Anne Moore and Graham D. Burrows, 'Hypnosis in the treatment of obsessive-compulsive disorder', *Australian Journal of Clinical & Experimental Hypnosis*, 19:2 (1991), 63–75. https://www.researchgate.net/publication/232448679_Hypnosis_in_the_treatment_of_obsessive-compulsive_disorder.

You can train your mind so it can *unconsciously* know how to improve your confidence or relaxation response in certain situations. In a word, you can begin to switch from conscious competence (having to think about something to do it well) to unconscious competence (not having to think about it). This is because the unconscious mind *knows* how to do things unconsciously. For example, you often don't need to think about walking, and so you can do things like walk and text, or walk and eat at the same time.

As well as various psychology studies showing its effectiveness, I also have several success stories of using guided mental rehearsal from my own coaching practice:

- Rick was able to go from being petrified of women to being able to talk to seventeen in one night
- Mika, an HR manager, managed to overcome her fear of writing reports (which used to cause her panic attacks)
- Harriet, a financial analyst, massively improved her presentation confidence and conquered her fear of public speaking

Some people are understandably sceptical about the power of hypnosis and guided imagery – especially because of some of the weird things out there, such as stage hypnotists turning people into chickens, or some 'woo-woo' practitioners claiming that they can take you back into your 'past lives' with hypnosis. But just for a moment, I want you to put aside your prejudices and try something: I want you to really focus and consciously imagine the following:

Now, you know what a lemon looks like, right? Well, see if you can imagine one in your mind's eye – a big yellow lemon – and really consciously imagine it … Now imagine taking a

knife, and cutting the lemon open, and, as you do so, the
smell of lemon wafting up into your nose ... Now take the
lemon slice in your mouth ... you may be able to feel the juicy
slice in your mouth as you do this ... and bite down on it ...
As you do so, a bit of zingy and sour lemon juice slowly oozes
out into your mouth ... it 'zings' the tip of your tongue ...

So, did your mouth water at all? Could you taste, smell or even
feel the lemon in your mouth, even slightly? If so, congratulations, you've just had a hypnotic experience! I haven't put a
lemon in your mouth at all; you've just used your imagination.
However, keep in mind that those who are autistic can struggle with hypnosis,* and that I haven't done a proper hypnotic
induction. But what I wanted to demonstrate here is the power
of using your imagination – which all of us human beings have
as an innate resource. If any of my clients ask, 'Does hypnosis
work?', I do the above exercise with them, and they are pleasantly surprised when they can taste the imaginary lemon. If
they don't like the taste, I have them imagine next they are
drinking a sweet molten hot chocolate that warms the inside of
their mouth to wash away the taste!

It should also be noted that memory can induce hypnosis.
When you access certain memories, you can re-experience the
sensations and feelings that you had at the time. Of course, you're
not *actually* there, but your brain can hypnotise you and make
you feel like you're re-experiencing certain memories, especially
those with strong emotions attached. For example, thinking of
a sad memory can trigger feelings of sadness, or thinking of a
memory of eating your favourite food may cause you to start sali-
vating. This is in fact how post-traumatic stress disorder (PTSD)
works; talking about memories or seeing something that reminds

---

* As a Christian I believe hypnosis, like a Swiss Army knife, is in and of itself
neither good nor bad – it's how you use it that matters.

you of the trauma causes a pattern match to a disturbing memory. In some cases, you may feel like you're reliving or re-experiencing that disturbing memory (known as 'emotional flashbacks').

There's a reason why solution-focused therapy and coaching schools, such as Human Givens College, Fusion Therapeutic Coaching and Uncommon Knowledge, all teach hypnotic and mental rehearsal for issues such as OCD, anger management and overcoming phobias – *because it works*. So, if you are still struggling to take that first step, then try doing some guided relaxation followed by some mental rehearsal of you taking that first step. You might find that after you finish mental rehearsal, you *intuitively* know how to take that next step. Of course, it may be useful to do some guided hypnosis or guided imagery with a coach or therapist.

GROWTH ACTION

Relax and rehearse your way to success

1. i) Ask yourself what the next smallest step is towards your goal(s).
    ii) Next, take five minutes to close your eyes and imagine yourself feeling calm, confident and relaxed as you take that next step, and feeling *really* good about taking it. Perhaps notice what other tiny actions you take along the way, as well as what's different about you as you do so.

2. Go to nickhatter.com/relax and listen to at least one guided relaxation recording.
3. Go to nickhatter.com/rehearse and listen to one guided rehearsal.

How can you make it more fun?

One thing that you may find helpful for taking that next small-est step is to make boring activities more fun. When doing the laundry, or going out for my daily walk, I might listen to an audiobook or a podcast. I also literally cannot work out without music. You can also turn anything into a game. For example, if you were starting a company, you could make a game to see how many 'no's you can get from early customers or investors! As for boring tasks like tax returns or accounting, you could make that into a game too: 'How low can I get my tax bill?'* Even while writing *The 7 Questions*, I would sometimes notice the potential for procrastination to come in; I would feel a bit stuck and think, *Where the hell do I go from here?* So, I would play a mental game for myself to see how high I could get the daily word count, especially on days I didn't feel like writing. I thought it would perhaps lead to me writing a load of nonsense. But I would often find that 'nonsense' ended up being something half-decent! In any case, there may be other ways you can make that smallest step or task much more fun! Use your imagination.

In a nutshell

What a journey this has been! We have covered a lot of ground in this book, including how low self-esteem is formed, funda-mental human needs, driving forces behind bad habits, deeply held unconscious motivations and hidden relationship patterns, core priorities, spiritual well-being and how to break free of pro-crastination. If you feel you've forgotten anything, feel free to go back over this book again – there's a lot of information in here.

---

* Of course, I am only joking here – taxes are an important valuable contribution to society that pay for vital services – but you get the idea.

Often behind procrastination is usually overwhelm, perfectionism, not knowing where to begin, and, sometimes, even trauma. Ultimately, the best way to kill procrastination is by taking tiny steps. If you're not sure what to do next, ask yourself, 'What's the next smallest step I can take?' – and then take it, no matter how small. In fact, *the smaller the better*. Remember that thinking of big tasks, especially in a stressed-out or anxious state of mind, can make even the smallest step seem like climbing mountains, which can lead to procrastination, as can outrageously high standards. As Australian public health doctor and lawyer Dr Marie Bismark says: 'Instead of asking "Will it be comfortable?" ask "Will I be glad I did it?" Works for everything from saying "yes" to going for a run, speaking up against injustice, filing your taxes, swimming under waterfalls, and stargazing at midnight.'

Also remember to utilise the power of mental rehearsal, which is your mind's virtual reality simulator; you can rehearse breaking through procrastination using your imagination.

If you're completely stumped as to what your next smallest step could be after reading *The 7 Questions*, here are some suggestions:

- Complete just *one* Growth Action in this book that you like the sound of (any one!)
- Complete the Emotional Needs Audit in Chapter 2
- Do just fifteen minutes of guided relaxation as this will help calm your amygdala and will help you to think clearer and more logically. Go to nickhatter.com/relax
- Take an Enneagram assessment to see your primary unconscious motivation (nickhatter.com/enneagram)
- Try a 12-Step Recovery group meeting (see the list of support groups in the Appendix) – keep in mind that each meeting has its own 'vibe', so make sure you try a few before deciding it isn't for you

- Hire a life coach or a therapist (you can learn more about me at nickhatter.com; you can also check out nickhatter.com/support)

Remember to use *The 7 Questions*

Whatever challenge you are facing in your life, remember to first consult your 7-question toolkit. These questions will help resolve most of life's common problems, as well as potentially unseen problems.

1. *How did I form my opinion of myself?* – If you're experiencing low self-esteem, look within using the tools in Chapter 1 to discover what has led to a low opinion of yourself (reminder: looking for interpretations that don't involve you for negative events, and vice versa for positive events, will help boost your self-esteem!).

2. *Am I lacking any fundamental needs?* – If you're feeling low, anxious or depressed, see if there's any innate human needs you're lacking and work on getting them met. Just as plants need sunlight and water, humans have needs too. Whatever needs you are lacking, ask yourself how you can start getting them met in healthy ways.

3. *Am I running from anything?* – Are you finding yourself slipping back into 'bad habits'? If so, remember to use this question to have a think about what is making it seem tempting. Remember that resentment, fear, shame, trauma, as well as unmet needs (which includes self-esteem), can make us want to retreat into our bad habits for relief.

4. *What's my hidden motivation?* – In all that you do, as well as in dating, friendships and interacting with people, always ask yourself this question and be totally honest with yourself. This will help you avoid sleepwalking through life as well as destructive relationship patterns.

5. *What's most important to me?* – Whether you're deciding between two pairs of shoes, two different career paths or various different options, this question will rapidly help you find what needs to be prioritised, and, in turn, will help you make better decisions and faster. Remember to also ask if you're over (or under) prioritising yourself.

6. *Are my beliefs serving me?* – If you're going through a tough time, or suffering from depression, then you need to have a look at your existential beliefs, for these can be a vital source of meaning and purpose as well as hope for the future.

7. *What's the next smallest step I can take?* – This question will help you break through procrastination, whether it's for sorting your life out, a big project or getting into shape. And, of course, sometimes the smallest step might be to just *relax* so that you can think more clearly and feel better.

Remember that often the answers are within, just waiting to be revealed. And by asking and answering the right questions, you can raise your self-awareness, discover who you truly are and live more consciously, which, in turn, will help you unlock your full potential.

Acknowledgements

I would like to thank the following people who made *The 7 Questions* possible:

My mum – my unofficial mentor and life coach throughout my coaching journey. All is forgiven. Thank you for supporting me.

My best friend, Steve – thanks for all the laughs and keeping me sane. Remember that it is a sick world and a sick society!

The FDBK team – for helping me scale up my coaching practice and supporting me with this book. Five stars for all of you!

Chris Thackery of Westbourne Grove Church – thank you for being a great source of support and a stellar example of a human being.

My agent, Jonathan Pegg – who spent much time with me, helping me craft and sell a compelling proposal and advance the creative vision of this book. None of this would have been possible without you!

My editor, Holly Harley at Piatkus Books (Little, Brown Book Group) – thank you for helping me shape this book into its full potential, and for your supportive, constructive and extremely useful feedback!

My fellows in 12-Step Recovery – you have saved me more times than I can count. It is an honour to serve and to be supported by you.

My business mentors, Brewster Barclay and Simon Stockley, who I met at Cambridge Judge Business School. Thanks for your generosity and wisdom over the years. I have learned much from both of you.

My therapeutic coaching supervisor and trainer, Frances Masters, founder of Fusion Therapeutic Coaching. You continue to teach me much!

Julia Kellaway, former commissioning editor at Penguin Random House – thank you for editing the earliest versions of the initial chapters, and for the moral support in my author journey!

Robin Harvey and Matthew Coleman at Pan Macmillan – thank you for scouting me and getting me noticed by top literary agencies.

My godmother Joan – you are my guardian angel. Thank you for all of your wisdom, love and support from my birth to my adult life.

Denise Winn, editor of *Human Givens Journal*, and Jane Tyrrell, director of Human Givens College, for their support and contributions for Chapter 2. Thank you!

Dr James Pitchford and Dani Kramer of Mathys & Squire LLP, for their generous and diligent work on FDBK.

Ed Turner of Berlad Graham LLP – thank you for being my 'legal eagle', and also a good laugh!

My abusers and bullies – you meant it for evil, but it worked out for my highest good. Hurt people hurt people. All is forgiven.

The homeless people of London – thank you for allowing me to be of service and helping me to feel useful. You are worthy.

Thank you to Vera, Rose and all the staff at The Gloria Palace Royal in Gran Canaria for their kind hospitality while I was writing *The 7 Questions*.

Uncle John – you probably repeated the trauma inflicted upon you as a child. All is forgiven. I hope one day you will be at peace.

And finally, thank you to my creator for helping restore me to sanity and for turning the evil I endured into something more than I ever dreamed possible.

Appendix

Do I need a life coach or therapist?

The answer is simple: it depends on what the life coach and therapist are trained in. The reality is that the line between coaching and therapy is very blurry. Typically, life coaching tends to be much more solution-focused and brief (i.e. you get results in twelve weeks, rather than one year), and tends to be more forward focusing. This is what makes it much more attractive than traditional therapy. Visit www.nickhatter.com/life-coaching-vs-therapy to find out more.

How do I become a life coach?

Becoming a life coach is one of the most rewarding journeys I have ever done. It's taught me so much about myself and humans. To me being a life coach is more than 'just a job'; it's a passion, a calling, and a service to humanity. If you'd like to follow in my footsteps and become a life coach yourself, visit www.nickhatter.com/training for more information.

What's this FDBK you've mentioned?

In case you missed it: FDBK is a healthy relationship and dating app that coaches you with peer feedback data on your dating profile, and also rewards you with virtual currency for giving feedback to others. This currency can then be spent on premium features in the app. FDBK is like having your very own dating and relationship coach in your pocket. See www. fdbk-app.com.

Challenging Catastrophising Exercise

When we catastrophise, we often have 'slippery slope' thinking. For example: 'My boss is upset with me' => I am homeless. In reality, it is more like this: 'My boss is upset with me' => (lots of other preceding events and choices) => I am homeless.

One way to challenge this type of thinking is to – after taking a moment to breathe and calm yourself down – break down what the preceding events are specifically and, at each event, come up with a plan as to what you would for each event. We panic because we think we have no other options and we don't think through the actual chain of events and choices.

For example, your boss may be upset with you, and this could lead to a difficult conversation, a performance review meeting, or, in the worst case, loss of a job. In the best case, it may lead to an honest and open conversation, which results in a much closer relationship and, as a result, you could get a promotion.

What would you do in the event of a difficult conversation, a performance review meeting or losing your job? In the last case, you would probably simply look for another job. In a performance review meeting, you might bring professional representation with you as well as make a case for why you are a good employee.

We often have more options than we realise, and we need not panic. We can create and implement action plans for each risk and event – a bit like doing a risk analysis for your own life! When you see that there are options you can choose, and measures you can take to prevent the worst-case scenario, you will see just how unlikely the worst-case scenario really is and, as a result, this can help calm down your catastrophic thinking.

1. **When do I usually catastrophise? What triggers do I have?**
   E.g. When I think my financial security is threatened.

2. **One situation where I currently catastrophise is:**
   E.g. When my boss schedules a meeting with me.

3. **What are the WORST, BEST and PROBABLE cases for this situation?**

WORST case	**BEST** case	**PROBABLE** case
E.g. I get fired, I become homeless and broke.	*E.g. I get promoted, a pay rise and a new car!*	*E.g. My boss simply has another project for me.*
AND THEN ...	*My family can then afford to upgrade to a better house!*	
I will struggle financially.		
AND THEN ...		
I will have to file for bankruptcy.		
AND THEN ...		
I will have to leave London because it's too expensive.		

WORST case   **BEST case**   **PROBABLE case**

AND THEN ...

*I will appear as
a failure!*

AND THEN ...

*Nobody will hire me
any more ...*

AND THEN ...

*I will never have
another job ...*

4. What constructive actions could I take to reduce
   my fear right now?

   *E.g. Guided relaxation to calm down first – and then perhaps
   email my boss to ask what the agenda is for our meeting.*

5. For each worst-case scenario (in Column 1):

i) What will I do if this DOES happen?

   *E.g. If I get fired, I will immediately begin looking for another
   job and registering with job search agencies.*

   *If I struggle financially, I will sell any unnecessary posses-
   sions (such as jewellery, or second car), and perhaps move to
   a smaller and cheaper place. I would also go to the benefits
   office if need be to ask for financial support in supporting
   my children.*

If I have to file for bankruptcy, I will seek legal advice from Citizens Advice Bureau.

If I have to leave London, I will move to Bath or Bristol.

ii) **What could I do to make this scenario LESS likely?**
   E.g. I will do regular professional development to keep my performance up at work. To avoid struggling financially, I will start cutting back on unnecessary expenses and start saving £100 a month. If I really struggle, I will seek professional financial advice and agree lower repayments with my creditors.

List of 12-Step Recovery Groups

If you follow the Growth Actions in this chapter, then you will have already made great progress on your fourth step, should you decide to pursue 12-Step Recovery as an option. Note that there are 12-Step support groups covering pretty much any problem, including:

- Alcoholics Anonymous (AA)
- Narcotics Anonymous (NA)
- Overeaters Anonymous (OA) – covers anorexia too
- Workaholics Anonymous (WA) – covers work avoidance too
- Underearners Anonymous (UA)
- Debtors Anonymous (DA)
- Friends and Family of Alcoholics (Al-Alon)
- Family and friends of Addicts Anonymous (FamAnon)
- Sex Addicts Anonymous (SAA)
- Love Addicts Anonymous (LAA)
- Sex and Love Addicts Anonymous (SLAA)

- Adult Children of Alcoholics and Dysfunctional Families (ACoA)
- Anorexics and Bulimics Anonymous (ABA)
- Gamblers Anonymous (GA)
- Nicotine Anonymous (NicA)
- Caffeine Anonymous (CAFA)
- Cocaine Anonymous (CA)
- Emotions Anonymous (EA)
- Co-dependents Anonymous (CoDA)
- Co-addicts* of Sex Addicts (CoSA)
- Co-addicts of Work Addicts (WorkAnon)

---

* A 'co-addict' is someone who has become 'addicted' to trying to fix, manage or control someone who has an addiction.